P9-AAY-728

Leading Professional Learning Teams

A Start-Up Guide for Improving Instruction

SUSAN E. SATHER

Foreword by
Shirley M. Hord

A JOINT PUBLICATION

CORWIN
A SAGE Company

education
northwest

MSA

For information:

Corwin
A SAGE Company
2455 Teller Road
Thousand Oaks, California 91320
(800) 233-9936
Fax: (800) 417-2466
www.corwinpress.com

SAGE Ltd.
1 Oliver's Yard
55 City Road
London, EC1Y 1SP
United Kingdom

SAGE India Pvt. Ltd.
B 1/I 1 Mohan Cooperative
Industrial Area
Mathura Road, New Delhi
India 110 044

SAGE Asia-Pacific Pte. Ltd.
33 Pekin Street #02-01
Far East Square
Singapore 048763

Printed in the United States of America.

Library of Congress Cataloging-in-Publication Data

Sather, Susan E.
Leading professional learning teams : a start-up guide for improving instruction / Susan E. Sather; foreword by Shirley M. Hord, a Joint Publication With the American Association of School Administrators and Education Northwest.
     p. cm.
Includes bibliographical references and index.
ISBN 978-1-4129-6552-1 (cloth)
ISBN 978-1-4129-6553-8 (pbk.)

  1. Teachers—In-service training. 2. Professional learning communities. 3. Teacher effectiveness. 4. Effective teaching. I. Title.

LB1731.S28 2009
370.71'55—dc22   2009017326

This book is printed on acid-free paper.

09 10 11 12 13 10 9 8 7 6 5 4 3 2 1

Acquisitions Editor:	Debra Stollenwerk
Associate Editor:	Julie McNall
Production Editor:	Libby Larson
Copy Editor:	Jeannette McCoy
Typesetter:	C&M Digitals (P) Ltd.
Proofreader:	Theresa Kay
Indexer:	Terri Corry
Cover Designer:	Lisa Riley
Graphic Designer:	Rose Storey

Contents

List of Figures and Tables

Foreword

For decades, school improvers have searched for the silver bullet—looking for a program, process, or innovation that could be put into place—to immediately exhibit desired outcomes.

By and large, these improvers have failed to give appropriate attention to "the giant leap" of implementation (Hall & Hord, 2006), where a great deal of knowledge and understanding of the innovation and of the persons who will use it are required. In the first paragraph of this book in the Preface, Susan Sather points out that this manuscript is committed to support both the planning and *implementation* of professional learning teams. Bravo, Susan. You are responding to this vital need.

Change process research and staff development research inform us of the complex work that is necessary for putting innovations or new programs into place. First, a clear mental image of what the new *thing* will look like when it is implemented in a high quality way is needed. Typically, such pictures of the program are fuzzy—in a word, ill defined. Unfortunately, such is the current state of professional learning communities or teams whose descriptions are ill defined. Many people who report about their PLTs indicate that their teams meet, period. Well, meeting is a necessary first step, but only a first step. This mental picture of PLTs will not lead us very far. Of course, there is not just one way or picture of a PLT, but there are models that are more productive and effective than others.

Linda Lambert (2003) defines the work of teams: "Teams are reciprocal learning communities in which each member expects to learn from and contribute to the development of others" (p. 26). Examining the three words—*professional, learning, team*—surely gives us clear understanding about what the teams are doing when they are in community: learning. But what are the teams learning? Their focus of attention is on student needs and how the staff will learn new content, strategies, and approaches so that they increase their effectiveness and students learn successfully. Sather gives the reader abundant information and insight about what the PLT is doing when it is meeting and learning, the skills that the members need, and the support structures and resources required. More important, one section is devoted to the role of the school administrator as leader and the responsibilities they have for supporting the teams in their work. The development of teacher leadership is also given attention so that leadership is broadened and deepened. Furthermore, the professionalism of teachers is strengthened when leadership opportunities and support are shared with them.

One of the major issues of implementation over the last three decades has been the lack of continuous quality professional development scheduled over time, with follow-up and coaching as a part of the work. Staff development researchers Bruce Joyce and Beverly Showers (2002) point out that just telling or reporting about a new program or practice will productively influence only 10 percent of the audience. Adding modeling and demonstrating increases the percentage, but giving the opportunity for practice and feedback ups the ante considerably to about 60 percent. But what really enables individuals to implement well is the follow-up and small-group or individual coaching to solve the individual user's problems. When this is supplied, typically 90 plus percent of the participants experience quality transfer of practice to the classroom.

Of what relevance is this to the leaders of the PLTs? A great deal. For not only does the PLT determine the learning that it needs to acquire in order to be more effective in supporting students to be more successful learners, but the PLT members will determine how they will go about doing the learning. Understanding how adults learn more productively so that their learning is transferred to their classrooms guides the PLT in designing its learning strategies.

The PLT is a self-governing body and as such will of necessity develop many skills and competencies that support their work as a learning community. It is here that Sather's guide is so helpful. There is a plethora of activities and opportunities for the PLT members to develop the skills necessary to operate effectively in their PLT. The guide "assists in building support structures and relationships, reinforcing PLT skills, and anticipating some of the potential challenges" (see Preface).

More important and in addition, the PLT context is one in which its members learn to use 21st-century skills being demanded of our public school graduates. These skills are critical thinking, problem solving, collaboration and teamwork, self-generative learning, quality communication, plus others. Because the PLT is a self-organizing group, these skills are required and are learned by the group. As the adults develop and experience the skills, they learn how to provide opportunities for students to develop them as well.

In the school, it will be important for all the teams to meet periodically and frequently as a whole staff. In this way, the staff members are studying school-wide data to identify learning needs of students. Staff then determine on what they will focus so that their learning enhances their capacity to address the students' needs across the school. Such goals would likely be consistent with the school improvement plans for the school. In this way, the PLTs support not only their specific grade level or academic subject areas but also a common purpose across the school.

This book serves the novice PLT leaders and members very well as well as those who are more experienced. Susan Sather and her colleagues in the partnering schools are congratulated for their work of experiencing, reviewing, and revising the rich array of materials in this book. They will prove valuable to all those interested in improving the quality of teaching, and thus, the successful learning of students in our schools.

Shirley M. Hord, PhD
Scholar Laureate
National Staff Development Council
August 2008

Preface

The most successful PLT in this building is run by the social studies department. They really got on board. They've structured their departmental meetings completely using the PLT structure. They have jumped in, read everything, even if they need to meet at lunch time. They've changed their practice—every single social studies teacher has changed practice around the PLT model. . . . PLTs are the vehicle we used to pull people together and create camaraderie. Were PLTs completely responsible for building cohesion? No, but they played a big part in that.

Lonnie Barber, Former High School Principal
Current Assistant Superintendent, Idaho

There is a body of research describing professional learning communities and documenting the positive effects of teacher collaboration in professional learning communities. However, there is much less information providing guidance for schools hoping to develop and sustain such communities. This publication was written as a resource for school administrators, school leadership teams, and teacher leaders as they embark on the journey establishing professional learning teams (PLTs) as a structure to enhance teacher collaboration and student learning in their schools. The main purpose is to help leaders understand and support the work of PLTs. This guide provides practical and useful information to assist them in planning, starting, and sustaining PLTs. It also assists central office administrators to understand and support the PLT process in their district's schools. At the same time, the research informing PLTs is included as a necessary underpinning to the leaders' information base.

School leaders are more fully equipped to provide essential supports when they understand the structure and processes of PLTs along with the rationale and research. Attending PLT workshops, engaging in training activities, and strengthening their own leadership skills are all important actions for these leaders. The PLT process described in this book provides guidance and strategies for teachers as well as school leaders to begin to effectively develop these learning communities in coordination with their school improvement plans. To ensure successful implementation, school leaders need support in taking the critical and sometimes difficult first steps toward creating job-embedded, collegial, schoolwide professional growth opportunities. This book provides that support with both a theoretical foundation for PLTs and concrete advice on getting ready for PLTs. It assists in building support structures and relationships, reinforcing PLT skills, and anticipating some of the potential challenges.

PLC VS. PLT

Professional Learning Communities (PLC) were evident in 2001 when we started developing the process referred to in this book as Professional Learning Teams (PLT). While there were descriptions of PLCs, at that time, there was no clear process for bringing teachers together to support the development of a community of learners focused on professional practice. Our belief was that a team approach would build a solid foundation, thus our goal was to provide a structure and tools to support teacher teams and connect it to the concept of professional learning. It is easier to build small *mini-communities* (teams) where individuals can share and learn from each other than to engage an entire school community all together in collaborative learning. We strongly recommend that all teams come together several times a year to share their work and maintain the connection to the larger community. However, most of the real work and transformation takes place in the smaller teams (PLTs), with the planned whole school sharing providing powerful touchstones for the entire staff, the overarching PLC.

While the term *PLC* is frequently used both in the literature as well as in practice in schools, we continue to use PLT to emphasize the importance of teachers working in smaller groups or teams in order to accomplish the work with a focus on their own specific students.

DESIGN AND DEVELOPMENT

The tools and strategies presented in this book were developed during the five-year period, 2001–2005, by a team of trainers, coaches, and curriculum specialists at the Center for School and District Improvement, part of the Northwest Regional Educational Laboratory (NWREL) in Portland, Oregon. In 2009, NWREL changed the name to Education Northwest. References to NWREL in this publication refer to work that was accomplished prior to the name change.

We sought to create tools for educators working in a standards- and data-driven educational system and to help support schools and teachers working to develop powerful teaching and learning through PLTs. The publication responds to the demands of the No Child Left Behind Act in assisting teachers to improve instruction in ways that increase learning and achievement for all students. These tools are continually refined and additional strategies developed in response to current needs in real schools. As a result, this is a revision of the first publication *Improving Instruction Through Professional Learning Teams* (2005) published by NWREL.

Six high-needs schools around the Northwest partnered with NWREL in honing the material presented here. During the pilot-test phase at these sites, particular attention was paid to the needs of school leaders to effectively support the PLT work. This field-based development allowed us to connect with partner-site leaders and combine their experience and knowledge with our own. Through the development process, we learned that the PLT process addresses the following school reform needs:

- Building stability and breadth in a school's instructional leadership by distributing leadership across the school through the use of teacher-led teams

- Developing staff collaboration as an important tool for improving the instructional programs in schools by using professional learning teams to improve teacher knowledge and teaching skills
- Aligning staff professional development with the school's improvement needs and objectives

The PLT process and materials align with the National Staff Development Council's standards for staff development (NSDC, 2001). (See Resource A for the complete text of the NSDC Standards for Staff Development.) In particular, this guide supports the following NSDC context standards aimed at improving the learning of all students:

- Organizes adults into learning communities whose goals are aligned with those of the school and district (Learning Communities)
- Requires skillful school and district leaders who guide continuous instructional improvement (Leadership)

In addition, the PLT process responds directly to a need identified by superintendents, principals, and teachers in the 2008 regional needs survey conducted by NWREL. That survey identified creating more opportunities (time) for teacher collaboration around school improvement as a high-priority concern, especially in larger districts (Leffler, 2008). The survey results indicate that they are seeking research-based information on how to create conditions that encourage teachers to collaborate around instructional practices in order to improve student learning and close achievement gaps. This includes finding flexible non-instructional time when teachers are able to engage in on-the-job professional development. A recent study in Washington State on barriers to raising student achievement also identified the need for "[t]ime for professional development and teacher-collaboration" as one of the top four barriers that, if removed, could make a positive impact on student achievement (Kruger, Woo, Miller, Davis, & Rayborn, 2008, p. i).

HOW TO USE THIS GUIDE

This is not a step-by-step, *how to create and manage a PLT* manual. Instead, it provides necessary background information and research needed to support the process. It also contains suggestions to guide the planning process along with some tools useful in early implementation. Rather than reading the guide from cover to cover, we recommend that you skim the pages, noting the contents, so that you can refer back to important information when the time and context provide the impetus to delve more deeply into the topic.

One question for school leaders to address up front is, "Are we ready to undertake PLTs as a change effort?" The information included in the guide will assist you in preparing to embark on the PLT process. It will also help you prepare the entire staff to support each other as you collectively engage in professional learning that enhances instructional practices.

This guide will help school leaders have meaningful discussions and learn together, using and modeling some of the PLT strategies and tools. Each chapter begins with a set of questions indicating main points within the chapter to focus the reader. Each chapter also ends with a brief summary of "key points" from the chapter as well as a set of questions to guide leadership team discussions and space for notes. The book concludes by describing potential challenges to the process that we encountered during field testing and evaluating the process as well as from our subsequent experience in conducting training in schools. Recommended reading and other resources are found at the end of the book.

The following graphics indicate special features to aid in these activities.

Action: Suggested points to use information and take action as you plan and implement PLTs in your school.

Voices From the Field: Direct quotes from school leaders that provide insights from actual PLTs.

Tool: Materials—handouts, transparencies, or posters—that can be reproduced and used to organize and introduce information on PLTs. The full-page masters can be found in the resource section at the end of the book.

The PLT Rubric (Tool H-12) can assist teams to self-assess their progress as they implement the process.

The Getting Started Roadmap (Tool H-13) contains the basic information found in the book in abbreviated form to assist busy school leaders in introducing and reviewing the process with staff. Intended as a synopsis tool for leaders, it contains abbreviated material from each chapter with the research base omitted to streamline the information.

Leadership Team Discussion: Suggestions at the end of each chapter to guide discussion among school leaders as you prepare to implement PLTs.

CHAPTER SUMMARIES

Chapter 1 describes PLTs in more detail and provides the rationale for developing and supporting them. Chapter 1 contains a sample timeline for the first year of PLT development. It shows how PLTs align with the features of effective professional development described in the research. It also describes other models for collaboration. This chapter is useful for school leaders as they plan for the PLT process and prepare to explain PLTs to district leaders, parents, staff, and community members.

Chapter 2 discusses preparing for successful PLT implementation. This includes assessing current conditions and teachers' readiness to engage in collaborative activities as well as understanding change. There is a focus on building relationships—developing trust, working with conflict, and ensuring productive avenues for communication.

Chapter 3 provides information about necessary structures—advocating for PLTs, using a leadership team, allocating time for professional development, making data available, aligning PLT efforts with school improvement goals, and ensuring accountability. Resource D contains additional suggestions for finding the necessary time for PLT members to attend workshops and meet as teams.

Chapter 4 presents research on the importance of both principal and teacher leadership and their relationship to student achievement. The role of the principal in supporting PLTs as well as the need to develop instructional leadership is discussed. This chapter also looks at facilitative and shared leadership as well as sustainable leadership. The chapter ends with a vignette describing a PLT in action—one school's experience implementing PLTs.

Chapter 5 considers factors supporting the success of PLTs, including ways that school leaders support and reinforce the teams' work. Emphasis is placed on ensuring that teams are led by teachers. A rubric is introduced to assist leaders and teams in understanding, reflecting, and self-evaluating the work of their PLT. Some of the possible challenges are mentioned with suggestions for addressing them. The chapter ends with the importance of celebrating success.

Acknowledgments

The original publication (2005) and this revision were made possible through the collaborative efforts of many individuals associated with NWREL. Former NWREL staff member Jennifer Jensen provided invaluable research and wrote an early review of the literature that served as a foundation for this publication. Dr. Jim Kushman, director of NWREL's Center for School and District Improvement, and Deborah Davis, Improving School Systems unit manager, along with former members of the Quality Teaching and Learning (QTL) Team, gave unfailing and ongoing support, encouragement, and advice. Those team members included Dr. Jerian Abel, Jacqueline Raphael, Mary Foulk, Kim Wier, Dr. Jayne Sowers, and Dr. Liliana Heller-Mafrica. Abel, Raphael, and Sowers also made significant written contributions to the professional learning teams training materials, as did Erin McGary-Hamilton at NWREL; Beverly Flaten, NWREL trainer; and Mike Sirofchuck from Kodiak High School in Alaska.

The QTL Advisory Committee, made up of practitioners and university professors, provided valuable advice and feedback that helped shape the content and format of PLT training as well as this guide: Abby Augustine, Judy Bieze, Betty Cobbs, Beverly Flaten, Maria Elena Garcia, Geoff Henderson, Dr. Esther Ilutsik, Alison Meadow, David Munson, Erik Running, Dr. Al Smith, and Sheila Wallace.

Several NWREL colleagues reviewed and influenced the first version of this guide: R. Newton Hamilton, Dr. Jim Leffler, and Katherine Luers. Other NWREL colleagues provided administrative support, insights, and additional assistance: Linda Gipe, Nancy Crain, Meg Waters, Sara Sellards, and Grant Menzies. Communications staff members provided editorial, bibliographic, and graphic design expertise for the original guide: Rhonda Barton, Linda Fitch, and Denise Crabtree continue to contribute their expertise.

External reviewers contributed their insights: Anne Jolly, SERVE; Becky Smith and Diane Appert, J.B. Thomas Middle School; Darrel Burbank, Holmes Elementary School; Dr. Diane Yendol-Hoppey, University of Florida; Dr. Lonnie Barber and Carol McCloy, Caldwell High School; Dr. Roberta Evans, University of Montana; and Linda Patterson, Gresham Barlow School District.

The author would like to express her deep gratitude to Debra Stollenwerk, Julie McNall, Libby Larson, and Jeannette McCoy at Corwin. Their ongoing guidance and patience helped shape this publication into a more complete and useful resource for school leaders.

Above all, I am grateful to the administrators and teachers in the schools that codeveloped the professional learning team process and strategies:

- Caldwell High School, Caldwell, Idaho
- Holmes Elementary School, Wilder, Idaho
- J. B. Thomas Middle School, Hillsboro, Oregon
- Kodiak High School, Kodiak, Alaska
- Shaw Middle School, Spokane, Washington
- Whittier Elementary School, Great Falls, Montana

Corwin gratefully acknowledges the contributions of the following reviewers:

Dr. Becky J. Cooke
Principal
Mead School District
Spokane, WA

Dr. Douglas Gordon Hesbol
Superintendent of Schools
Laraway CCSD 70C
Joliet, IL

Steve Knobl
High School Principal
Pasco County School System
Gulf High School
New Port Richey, FL

Mark White
Principal
Hintgen Elementary School
La Crosse, WI

About the Author

 **Dr. Susan E. Sather** has a PhD in Educational Administration from the University of California Berkeley and is a senior program advisor at Education Northwest in Portland, Oregon (formerly known as the Northwest Regional Educational Laboratory). She leads the Laboratory's Professional Learning Teams (PLT) work, supervising and conducting PLT training in schools around the nation. She also contributes to research on issues such as high school academic rigor. Dr. Sather has 38 years of experience in education, 17 as a teacher working with a dropout prevention program and in special education. Prior to joining NWREL, she was western regional manager and a staff developer for a whole-school reform model, Ventures Education Systems. She has conducted research and evaluation through the School of Education and the School of Social Welfare at the University of California Berkeley, and with ARC associates in Oakland, California. At ARC, she was a member of the Leading for Diversity research team and coauthor of *Leading for Diversity: How School Leaders Promote Positive Interethnic Relations* (2002).

Understanding Professional Learning Teams

School improvement is most surely and thoroughly achieved when teachers engage in frequent, continuous, and increasingly concrete and precise talk about teaching practice.

Judith Warren Little, 1991, p.12

FOCUS OF THIS CHAPTER

- What are professional learning teams (PLTs)?
  - PLT inquiry cycle
  - Sample timeline for one year
  - PLTs versus committees
- Why have PLTs?
  - Teacher collaboration influences student achievement.
  - High-quality teaching makes a difference in student learning.
  - Preservice training and classroom experience are not sufficient to develop high-quality teaching.
  - Traditional professional development is often insufficient to improve teaching quality.
  - Team-based professional learning improves teaching and learning.
- What are some features of effective professional development?
- What are some other models teachers use for collaboration?

DEFINING PROFESSIONAL LEARNING TEAMS ■

The need for teacher learning communities is now commonly accepted. These communities have multiple definitions with certain commonalities: teachers work collaboratively to reflect on their own practice, examine evidence about the relationship between practice and student outcomes, and make changes that improve teaching and learning for the particular students in their classes (McLaughlin & Talbert, 2006). Researchers and practitioners are now honing the definition of professional learning communities to provide more specificity and direction. In this publication, PLTs are defined as teams of four to six teachers from the same school, department, or grade level who come together to help each other improve student learning by changing classroom instruction. PLTs are goal oriented and maintain an unrelenting focus on student learning. PLTs assume that the needs of every student are not being fully met. This is not any one teacher's fault; however, all teachers share collective responsibility to address the problem.

PLT members collaboratively learn and improve practices together by doing the following:

- Examining and analyzing disaggregated student achievement and classroom data—this information guides decisions and choices around instructional practices that focus on improving student learning
- Selecting a specific area of student need to investigate as a focus for changing practice
- Framing an inquiry question to guide the PLT's work
- Investigating research-based strategies and best practices to increase their knowledge base and inform decisions about new practices to use in teaching their students
- Analyzing current teaching practices throughout the school to identify successful practices already in place as well as to understand schoolwide needs
- Determining specific areas for instructional change and trying out new strategies or honing existing practices that affect classroom learning
- Collecting classroom data to document activities and assess results
- Sharing personal practices and expertise through reflective dialogue, analysis of student work, and observing each other's classroom practices
- Functioning effectively as a team by paying attention to collaboration and documenting team activities
- Sharing the focus and results of each team's work with the greater school-wide community

Teachers in PLTs work together by doing the following:

- Meeting on a regular basis to support and learn from each other
- Sharing classroom practices with their colleagues
- Committing to improve their practice and supporting their colleagues in doing the same
- Seeking to improve their collaboration skills and applying them to effective PLTs and to the classroom

In PLTs, teams of teachers engage in activities to examine their current classroom practices and implement thoughtful change. PLTs work within their own content areas as well as school and district curriculum guidelines. The focus is on enhancing student learning and achievement by collaboratively examining and changing teaching practice. Ideally, the school staff is organized into small groups—PLTs—of four to six people, who "get to know and trust one another" (Jalongo, 1991, p. 73). Teams may be organized by grade level, content area, or specific interests that emerge from examining data. Interdisciplinary teams offer the opportunity for teachers to learn about different content areas and their specific ways of teaching. When teams collaborate to implement the same strategies in multiple content areas, students can benefit as they move from class to class or different grade levels as they bring an understanding of the process with them. The decision to form interdisciplinary teams or organize around some other appropriate factor, such as a department or common goal, should be made thoughtfully. Some schools also include vertical curriculum teams who meet less often but work together to assure articulation of goals and curricula from grade to grade in the entire school.

Ultimately, "teams are not necessarily permanent . . . they must be organized around shifting needs and problems to solve" (Louis & Miles, 1990, p. 24). Changes in team composition also need to be made thoughtfully for the purpose of enhancing the focus on student learning.

> *[T]he hallmark of any successful organization is a shared sense among its members about what they are trying to accomplish.*
>
> Susan J. Rosenholtz, 1989, p. 13

PLTs follow the process illustrated in Figure 1, PLT Inquiry Cycle on page 4. A full-page master of this cycle is included as Tool H-1 under Resources in the back of this book. An additional tool, H-2, includes the cycle with a brief explanation of each step.

For many schools, the first step in developing PLTs is a full-day workshop for the entire staff, ideally conducted in August before school starts. This workshop introduces the concept of PLTs and includes an examination of current achievement data to begin exploring what and how students are learning. Participants begin to identify specific student learning needs that will guide their inquiry. At this first meeting, teachers commonly form teams based on their interests. However, teams may also be formed based on content or grade level. Effective teamwork skills are introduced and reinforced in successive meetings.

After studying student data that relate to specific content and students, each team chooses to focus on a specific area of student need. Teachers then move to a critical examination of research and best practices. They also consider what and how teachers in their school are currently teaching. It is important to identify effective practices already in place that may be implemented by others as well as to understand schoolwide needs. Based on this information, each PLT chooses one or two new instructional strategies to try out in the classroom. The team decides how they will implement the practice or strategy and exactly what teachers will be doing in the classroom. They can collaboratively develop an implementation rubric so each team member is using the practice the same way. A crucial next step is deciding how to evaluate the effectiveness of each strategy by collecting and analyzing classroom data. At this point they may develop a common assessment so they can compare students' progress in all classrooms trying out the strategy. Finally, if the strategy proves effective,

TOOL

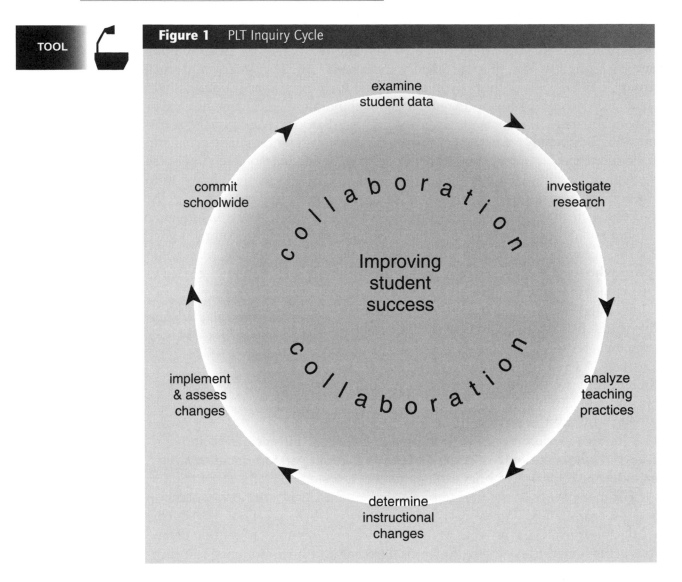

Figure 1   PLT Inquiry Cycle

examine
student data

commit
schoolwide

collaboration

Improving
student
success

investigate
research

Collaboration

implement
& assess
changes

analyze
teaching
practices

determine
instructional
changes

information is shared with the entire staff and they are asked to consider adopting one or more successful practices. The cycle is then repeated.

This inquiry cycle helps teachers and administrators develop a coherent vision of school change as they build a culture that values and uses data to inform decisions. At the same time, they increase clarity about desired outcomes and develop consistent accountability connected to student learning. When teachers start by examining schoolwide data and move to classroom-based data collection and analysis, their team inquiry is situated within a larger context of schoolwide inquiry. The teacher's repertoire is strengthened by investigating and employing best practices and research-based strategies. All this contributes to the development of a culture of professional learning within the school. PLTs are an important vehicle used to support schools as they reculture to become professional learning communities. PLTs also alter school culture from one of teacher isolation to collaboration and transparency around what goes on in classrooms.

Note: Periodic, schoolwide sharing brings teams together as an overarching PLT. While we place emphasis on teams working individually to focus efforts on their specific students, schoolwide meetings are essential to viewing teams as part of the entire school system. In fact, it is important to share the process and outcomes with other schools and the central office—the larger districtwide system. As one assistant superintendent in the Spokane district framed it, "These are not just my students in my classroom; I am responsible for all students in the school and ultimately for all students in this district, in fact in the state of Washington." In this way, improving student learning becomes an overarching goal or focus for the entire organization.

The schedule on pages 6 and 7 (Table 1) represents a suggested sequence for training and implementing PLTs during the first year. It includes both a description of the training and a column with suggestions for leaders to support PLT implementation. The timeline may vary with each school and is directly related to the amount of time available for PLTs to meet. Ideally, PLTs meet weekly or at least biweekly, and the process involves a series of workshops to train staff in the PLT tools and collaboration skills. In addition, teams meet individually between workshops to implement what they have learned.

PLTs vs. Committees

An important distinction needs to be made between PLTs and school committees. Both structures are important to the work of schools. However, PLTs focus directly on student learning and are aimed at improving students' academic success. Committees are often formed to focus on specific topics or needs within the school. For instance, a committee may be formed to deal with school safety, dress codes, student-discipline issues, and develop new policies around student behavior. While these issues are important to the school and help establish an environment conducive to student learning, the immediate focus is not aimed at improving student learning. PLTs should be encouraged to keep student learning at the center of their work as a team. A committee may disband when its work is complete. PLTs, on the other hand, may shift membership but need to become institutionalized as a way of doing business in a school.

> Teachers in professional learning communities are more likely to be consistently well informed, professionally renewed, and inspired so that they inspire students.
>
> Shirley Hord, 1997, p. 30

THE NEED FOR PLTs ■

Individuals, groups, and schools engage in professional learning for a number of purposes: acquiring new skills, stimulating intellect, engendering a sense of renewal, building a common vision, developing new curricula, or establishing and institutionalizing policies and procedures. *Leading Professional Learning Teams: A Startup Guide for Improving Instruction* assumes that the primary purpose of PLTs is to support teachers in improving student learning by changing their instruction. Other outcomes such as developing a collaborative school culture and honing teachers' leadership skills are additional benefits.

Table 1 Typical PLT Timeline for One Year

Task	School Staff	School Leaders
1. Determining PLT topics based on student data	• PLT process is introduced • Staff analyzes student achievement and other data to determine specific topics to investigate in order to improve classroom achievement • Teachers select into PLTs • Effective teamwork and collaboration skills are introduced	• Introduce the PLT process as a schoolwide effort • Provide data and ensure coordination with the district and school processes already in place • Attend all PLT training sessions • Intentionally build trust and create a safe environment for teachers • Acknowledge and celebrate past successes and build on them • Plan to celebrate often as long as there is cause for authentic celebration
2. Digging deeper into data and developing a focus question to guide inquiry	• Teams deepen their understanding of the topic based on further analysis of data • Teams share and discuss current practices • Each PLT develops a focus question to guide its inquiry	• Provide additional resources as needed • Understand the focus for each team—attend individual team meetings and read team logs • Provide avenues for teams to share information with the rest of the staff: provide time at staff meetings for sharing; ask teams to make notebooks public
3. Investigating research and best practices	• Discuss pertinent research and identify ways to access additional research related to the PLT's focusing question • Deepen understanding of current research and best practices, the schoolwide context, and implications for their own professional practice • Teams identify research-based instructional practices to implement	• Provide some research and information on best practices • Develop or expand the school's professional library • Model professional learning by sharing information from your own reading • Develop instructional leadership skills to support teachers in changing practice (see Chapter 4)
4. Analyzing teaching practices	• Teachers become reflective practitioners by using tools for structured reflection • Teams collect and share schoolwide data on current classroom practices and methods of assessment • Teams develop skills for systematically analyzing student work	• Develop visibility in classrooms; institute the walk-through practice • Listen to each teacher's voice and respond
5. Determining instructional changes	• PLTs review potential practices and select one or more to implement • Develop a common understanding on the characteristics and steps of the practices	• Schedule time for schoolwide sharing of selected practices and implementation plans • Create conditions that allow teachers to develop their own expertise and sense of empowerment

Task	School Staff	School Leaders
	• Discuss ways to monitor progress with these practices • Share progress with colleagues	• Support the development of teacher leadership • Remember to celebrate progress
6. Implementing and assessing changes	• Teams identify and evaluate specific classroom-based assessments to monitor new practices • Develop common classroom assessments • Implement new practices • Collect and evaluate classroom data to determine the impact on student learning • Draw conclusions and refine the new practice as needed	• Ensure access to assessment information • Provide guidance and feedback to teachers on observed changes • Provide release time so teachers can observe each other implementing the new teaching practice
7. Analyzing results	• Determine the effectiveness of new practices on improving student learning • Analyze and synthesize results from the implementation of new practices • Prepare a presentation for schoolwide sharing • Reflect on the PLTs work and accomplishments for the year	• Serve as a resource as needed • Assure access for teachers to computers and PowerPoint (or other software) to prepare presentations • Reflect on the Leadership team's work and accomplishments • Plan for year-end celebration
8. Committing schoolwide	• Present results to staff with a recommendation for schoolwide adoption—if the practice does not indicate student gains, speculate why and what changes might be needed • Each teacher commits to adopting one new practice for the coming school year • Identify support needed for schoolwide adoption	• Understand the strategies and results of each PLT • Provide time for schoolwide sharing • Facilitate staff discussion around practices and come to agreement on which practices will be valuable to implement schoolwide • Publicly celebrate the work and successes of every PLT • Begin to plan PLT implementation for the coming year

The research literature supports the positive link between team-based learning located in strong teacher learning communities and student achievement gains. Research is cited in subsequent sections addressing each of the following points:

- Professional learning communities do improve learning for students under certain conditions: when teachers collaborate as they reflect on their practice, examine the link between practice and student outcomes, and make changes in that practice to improve student learning.
- High-quality teaching is the most critical component for producing high-caliber learning in all students.

- Preservice education and classroom experience are linked to improved student learning; however, they are insufficient to maintain teachers' success in a rapidly changing educational environment.
  - The traditional methods for inservice education— coursework, institutes, formal workshops, and classroom experience—are important yet insufficient by themselves for creating *schoolwide* improvements in classroom practice and teacher quality.
  - PLTs provide an organizing structure for professional development leading to schoolwide improvement in teacher practice and student learning.

> *Even the highest-quality professional development resources will falter unless teachers can work together on new ideas and reflect on practice and its implications for students' learning.*
>
> Milbrey W. McLaughlin & Joan E. Talbert, 2006, p. 3

Teacher Collaboration Affects Student Learning

School-based teacher learning communities focused on improving student learning serve several functions. They provide opportunities for teachers to identify and respond to classroom-based problems affecting their own students. They connect teachers' work to the larger system context. They "provide opportunities for reflection and problem solving that allow teachers to construct knowledge based on what they know about their students' learning and evidence of their progress" (McLaughlin & Talbert, 2006, p. 5). Examining students' work together helps teachers understand the success or failure of the assignment and teaching practice. The learning team provides a forum for teachers to share resources as they translate knowledge gained from colleagues, research, university coursework, and other professional development into practice that is relevant to their specific students and classrooms.

McLaughlin and Talbert (2006) report on several studies providing statistical evidence that teacher community has a positive effect on student achievement gains (Lee & Smith, 1995; 1996; Lee, Smith, & Croninger, 1997). These studies indicate that students do better academically in schools where teachers take collective responsibility for the success of all students. That shared responsibility lies at the heart of the PLT process. Vescio and her colleagues (2006, 2008) reviewed the research on professional learning communities as a way to improve teacher practice and student achievement and found that such participation "impacts teaching practice as teachers become more student centered. In addition, teaching culture is improved because the learning communities increase collaboration, a focus on student learning, teacher authority or empowerment, and continuous learning" (2006, p. 18). They cite six studies connecting student learning outcomes and achievement to teacher collaboration; the success of these efforts depended on the intensity of their focus on student learning and achievement. However, student achievement gains did vary with the strength of the PLC in the school. Two studies (Supovitz, 2002; Supovitz & Christman, 2003) indicate that those communities producing significant gains in student learning engaged in "structured, sustained, and supported instructional discussions and investigated the relationships between instructional practices and student work" (Vescio et al., 2006, p. 87). Taken together, these studies point to the importance of focusing the work of a PLT on issues of student learning with a goal of enhancing achievement. At the same time, PLTs must honor the knowledge and experience of teachers as well as knowledge and theory generated by research.

Teacher Quality Translates to Student Learning

Teacher quality may well be the single most critical factor in addressing improved learning for all students. While many aspects of teacher quality are difficult to quantify, three credible measures exist:

1. The caliber and extent of a teacher's pre-service education

2. Assignment to the field in which a teacher is prepared

3. The inservice education of the teacher, both through classroom experience and formal learning opportunities

Teacher quality as defined by these indicators emerges as the primary factor that predicts students' learning gains and achievement. Darling-Hammond (1999) contends that more focus must be placed on improving teaching in order to meet continually rising standards. Furthermore, she stresses that supporting and using quality collaborative planning among teachers is paramount to achieving these goals. In fact, "the estimated difference in annual achievement growth between having a good teacher and a bad teacher can be more than one grade-level equivalent in test performance" (Mayer, Mullens, Moore, & Ralph, 2000, p. 5).

Placing well-trained teachers in assignments matching their fields of study is the second key component. "To be effective, teachers must know their subject matter so thoroughly that they can present it in a challenging, clear, and compelling way. They must also know how their students learn and how to make ideas accessible so that they can construct 'teachable moments'" (NCTAF, 1996, p. 6). In addition, teachers must consciously address the diversity of their students. "Issues related to race, culture, or class are among the biggest challenges for improving U.S. education in terms of both numbers of students addressed and persistent challenges in effectively serving these populations" (Boethel, 2003, p. 2). Teachers who get results with students not only know what they are teaching but also how best to teach that particular discipline to the specific students in their classrooms. They also strive to understand cultural differences and how those affect classroom climate and student learning. An increasing challenge for teachers in many areas is the influx of English language learners. Few higher education teacher preparation programs require more than a single multicultural class for mainstream teachers and many enter their first classroom lacking strategies for teaching multilingual and multiethnic students. This highlights the need for effective professional development for teachers to understand and address these issues.

Addressing pedagogy and content is an incomplete solution to the problem of teacher quality. Schools continue to be challenged to prepare students

Highly qualified teachers: To be deemed highly qualified, teachers must have the following:

1. *a bachelor's degree,*

2. *full state certification or licensure, and*

3. *prove that they know each subject they teach.*

U.S. Department of Education, 2005

It is assumed that the knowledge teachers need to teach well is generated when teachers treat their own classrooms and schools as sites for intentional investigation at the same time that they treat the knowledge and theory produced by others as generative material for interrogation and interpretation.

M. Cochran-Smith & S.L. Lytle, 1999, p. 272

[O]nly under certain conditions will teacher communities flourish into communities engaged in instructional improvement. . . . [P]articular kinds of teacher communities are needed: those that are focused on improving the instructional core of schooling and provided with the necessary strategies, structures, and supports.

Jonathan A. Supovitz &
Jolley Bruce Christman, 2003, p. 1

to participate in a rapidly evolving society. Incorporating technology into classrooms, moving to standards-based assessment, and addressing the needs of increasingly diverse students are only some of the challenges teachers face. The formal education of many teachers dates back 10 to 20 years or more. "Less than half of American teachers report feeling 'very well prepared' to meet many of these challenges" (Lewis et al., 1999, p. iii).

Without effective inservice education, the ability of teachers to understand and integrate changes into their practice erodes, as does their ability to evaluate the effects on their students' learning. Teachers working collaboratively need to develop their knowledge of practice around issues related to their own students' learning. When teachers fully engage in professional development focused on adding new skills and strategies to their repertoire as well as deepening their content knowledge, they move closer to becoming the "highly qualified teachers" called for in No Child Left Behind (NCLB).

Teachers Need More Than Classroom Experience

It stands to reason that classroom experience alone is not sufficient to improve teacher quality. Rosenholtz (1989) found a negative correlation between the years of classroom experience a teacher had and the students' gains in reading. In other words, the more experienced a faculty, the less likely students were to progress in reading. Wenglinsky (2000) found no correlation between teacher experience and student achievement in mathematics and science in the nationwide data of the National Assessment of Educational Progress.

There is, however, a strong positive correlation between teachers' beliefs about their own learning and their students' achievement. In the learning-impoverished schools studied by Rosenholtz (1989, p. 81), teachers felt that they became proficient teachers just by teaching—without any further attention to their professional learning, especially after an average of 4.5 years in the classroom. This belief is accurate but ironically only for those teachers and schools that do not subscribe to it. As Fullan (1991) points out, "Beginning teachers will get better or worse depending on the schools in which they teach" (p. 315). In schools that only equate teaching time with teacher quality, individual teacher quality is more likely to degenerate over time rather than improve. A school must already believe in attention to continuous teacher learning outside the classroom in order to promote positive professional development and teachers' collaboration (Rosenholtz, 1989). Experience does have an impact, but it is contingent upon the caliber of teaching and learning that surrounds the new teacher; it is not an inherent by-product of showing up and teaching every day.

Traditional Professional Development Is Often Insufficient to Improve Teaching Quality

If classroom experience alone does not equate to teacher quality, then the efficacy of teacher professional development becomes critical. Traditionally, classroom experience is supplemented with formal professional development focused on improving teaching and learning. These opportunities are sometimes structured around single events: an inservice training, a conference, or a summer institute. However, "change is a process, not an event" (Hall & Hord, 2001, p. 4).

Without professional development focused on enhancing teaching and learning, teachers often teach the way they were taught. "This is the method that they have seen the most, what they know best, and in which they have the most confidence" (Maeroff, 1993, p. 6). As teachers alter some of their teaching practices, they need to change some of their attitudes, beliefs, and connected behaviors. Teachers are currently being asked to raise their expectations for students' performance. This often means a radical shift in the way teachers are teaching. Asking people to change—to leave a comfort zone and stop doing some of the familiar things that they feel they do well and enjoy doing—can create a sense of sadness. What may be seen as resistance to change may well be grief "over the loss of favorite and comfortable ways of acting" (Hall & Hord, 2001, p. 5). Isolated events do not provide adequate support for the gradual and sometimes traumatic process of abandoning old behaviors and integrating new ones permanently into practice.

Ninety-nine percent of all teachers participate in some kind of professional development during a 12-month period. However, depending on the topic, one half to four fifths of this training "lasted from one to eight hours, or the equivalent of one day or less" (Lewis et al., 1999, p. v). Lewis and colleagues reported that as few as 8 percent of teachers identified strong results from these brief learning experiences. The same study found that when teachers spent more than eight hours studying a single topic, three to five times as many teachers reported their learning affected their classroom practices "a lot" (p. 29). Although teachers are being exposed to the kinds of topics consistent with educational reform movements, they sometimes experience that information in fragmented and superficial ways.

Professional developers and school leaders need to remember that adults, like children, perform best in a learner-centered environment that connects the focus of their study to their prior knowledge—experiences, interests, and strengths. Teachers need to understand the purpose for learning and have the opportunity to practice, evaluate, and adapt their learning to their individual contexts. A meta-analysis of nearly 200 educational research studies concludes that, in order for a training event to be successful, "combinations of four components (theory, demonstration, practice, and feedback) appear necessary to develop the levels of cognitive and interactive skills that permit practice in the classroom" (Showers, Joyce, & Bennett, 1987, p. 86). After the initial training, "teachers need social support as they labor through the transfer process" of integrating the new skill into their practice (p. 86). On average, "about 25 teaching episodes during which the new strategy is used are necessary before all the conditions of transfer are achieved" (p. 86). Pairing with an expert or peer coach for reflection and feedback between episodes ensured success for *nearly all* teachers. When PLTs use peer observation, they experience the opportunity for reflection and feedback. It is important to provide structured guidelines by using an observation protocol that creates a safe environment conducive to opening one's classroom to scrutiny. In other words, we are asking teachers to make their teaching public as they continue to learn and change practice.

> While teachers are being asked to engage their own students in active learning, problem solving, and inquiry, they rarely experience this kind of learning themselves.
>
> National Commission on
> Teaching and America's Future, 1996, p. 41

An increasing number of professional development programs contain these critical components, and some now provide the support and follow-up required for teachers to integrate new learning into actual classroom practice. Follow-up can come in the form of coaching, mentoring, lesson study, collaborative analysis of student work, and peer observation with constructive feedback. In their PLTs, teachers provide each other with encouragement and extended social support to apply new learning. They also assist teachers in understanding the theory and principles behind that learning and using those principles to adapt what they are learning to the unique contexts of each classroom. These conditions help ensure success for both teachers and their students.

> Teachers who spend more time collectively studying teaching practices are more effective overall at developing higher-order thinking skills and meeting the needs of diverse learners.
>
> Linda Darling-Hammond, 1998, p. 7

Team-Based Professional Learning Improves Teacher Quality

Neither traditional forms of professional development nor classroom experience can address teachers' learning needs by themselves. But combining both and enhancing that mixture with the crucial ingredient of collaboration can realize tremendous changes in teachers' beliefs and practices. Using inservice days, institutes, conferences, and coursework as methods of disseminating information has a permanent place in the staff development protocol (Wald & Castleberry, 1999). However, practical application of this information—teachers modifying their beliefs and classroom practices—requires that teachers have an ongoing opportunity to discuss, understand, and adapt it in the company of their colleagues.

Researchers have described the cultures of successful schools that are changing practice through high-quality professional development and realizing significant student learning gains. These schools have a strong resemblance to one another and are currently referred to as a *professional learning community*. Professional learning communities are characterized by the following:

- Reflective inquiry in a climate of trust, risk taking, and collaboration
- Shared philosophies such as working agreements or norms, values, and vision, as well as shared personal practices that illustrate the application of those values
- Skilled use of data for decision making
- A focus on student learning while demanding quality learning from all members of the school community—students, staff, parents, and administrators

Collaboration is the structure that supports achieving the other elements and outcomes of strong professional learning communities for students and staff. Ongoing teacher-to-teacher collaboration for the specific purpose of evaluating and improving classroom practice is essential (Bransford, Brown, & Cocking, 2000; McLaughlin & Talbert, 1993, 2006). Teams of teachers do get results. In looking for proof of effectiveness of teacher professional development, Borko (2004) found evidence that strong professional learning communities can foster teacher learning and contribute to instructional improvement and school reform. She concluded, "High quality professional development helps teachers deepen their knowledge and transform their teaching" (p. 5). The QUASAR (Quantitative Understanding: Amplifying Student Achievement and Reasoning) project also concluded that professional learning communities were central to fostering teacher change and student learning (p. 6).

Murphy and Lick (1998) cite one specific example of the type of change that they observed in working with faculty study groups:

> *The work of PLTs has transformed how our grade levels work together. It is now the culture of our school with all teachers on a PLT this year.*
>
> Cathy Carson, Principal, St. Helens, Oregon

The longer the teams experienced the study group mind-set (of learning teams) one period per week, the other planning periods became more like the study group time. As study groups became the norm at Elder Middle School, the dialogue[s] in the faculty lounge, in faculty meetings, and in department meetings were also noticeably different. Teachers talked about instruction . . . . We are a community of learners. The cumulative effect of this dynamic was also validated in the student data. (p. 86)

In eight schools studied by WestEd (2000), the crucial habit of collegial sharing became embedded in each school. Each school showed strong gains in relation to its school improvement goals. Professional development leading to those gains shared these common traits:

1. An array of professional development strategies built the knowledge and skill needed to carry out improvement goals.

2. Teachers learned in a variety of ways—formally and informally, from outside experts, building trainers, and from each other—and all forms contributed to growth.

3. Schools often started with formal learning in order to focus on specific content or to benefit from a particular learning structure.

4. While formal training often set the stage, the more informal modes accounted for new ideas taking root and becoming part of daily practice.

During field tests of the PLT process at five partner sites, NWREL found evidence that PLTs provided the following benefits:

- Teachers increased their awareness of or knowledge about instructional issues.
- Teachers and administrators increased their focus on student learning.
- Collective responsibility for student learning increased.
- Teachers made better use of research-based practices.
- Teachers experienced greater opportunities to exercise teacher leadership.
- The PLT process helped staff focus on overall school improvement issues.
- Collegiality and collaboration among teachers and administrators increased. (Raphael, 2005)

Effective professional development requires certain features. The PLT process is specifically designed to incorporate all six features of effective professional development linked to changes in teacher performance and/or student learning found in some of the more rigorous research studies (Cohen & Hill, 1998; Desimone, Porter, Garet, Yoon, & Birman, 2002; Garet, Porter, Desimone, Birman, & Yoon, 2001; Kennedy, 1998; Porter, Garet, Desimone, Yoon, & Birman, 2000). The six features and their links to PLTs are summarized in Table 2.

In addition to PLTs, there are several other models that engage teachers in working collaboratively. A common element among these models is the need to examine teaching practice with an eye to improving student learning. When teachers work together with this in mind, it makes a difference.

■ OTHER MODELS FOR TEACHER COLLABORATION

Strategies used to promote collaboration are often similar from model to model, and some resemble PLT strategies. We find that PLTs are compatible with many other forms of professional development. Schools that are engaged in using one or more of these models may choose to meld the PLT process with their current work.

Action Research

Action research engages teachers in ongoing inquiry into their own practice around teaching and learning. They may do this individually, in collaborative

Table 2 Features of Effective Professional Development

Feature	Description	PLT Applications
Form of activity (Desimone, Porter, Garet, Yoon, & Birman, 2002; Garet, Porter, Desimone, Birman, & Yoon, 2001)	The professional development activity spans a continuum from individual workshop attendance to participation in study groups. Effectiveness of the different forms depends on the context. Traditional workshops are less effective than teacher networks and ongoing study groups.	The PLT training includes a series of workshops with individual PLTs meeting regularly throughout the year to work through the inquiry cycle.
Collective participation and collaboration (Desimone et al., 2002; Garet et al., 2001)	Teachers from the same school, department, or grade level participate collectively in the professional development activity and collaborate to implement what was learned. Activities designed for teachers in the same school, grade, or subject area are more effective than programs that do not target teachers who work together.	By design, the PLT structure requires teachers to collaborate as they share their practice, choose strategies to try out in their classrooms, decide how to measure effectiveness, and discuss results first in their individual PLTs and later with the entire school.
Content /pedagogical focus (Cohen & Hill, 1998; Desimone et al., 2002; Garet et al., 2001; Kennedy, 1998)	The focus is on developing expertise in the subject or content areas teachers teach and on how students learn that subject. There is a focus on instruction that is targeted to the specific school and student context.	PLTs may be content specific or interdisciplinary as long as they focus on enhancing student learning by strengthening and/or changing teacher practice. Interdisciplinary teams can strengthen multiple content areas as teachers share knowledge.
Active learning (Desimone et al., 2002; Garet et al., 2001)	There are opportunities for teachers to engage actively in meaningful analysis of teaching and learning—both during and after formal professional development events.	Teachers engage actively in analyzing their own teaching and learning both during PLT workshops and in their individual PLTs. They read and discuss research; analyze student work; observe each other teaching; and receive feedback.
Sustained time and duration (Garet et al., 2001)	Professional development is sustained over time and involves a substantial number of contact hours. Longer, more sustained, and intensive professional development is more likely to make an impact than shorter activities.	PLTs are structured to receive eight to nine days of training during the first year of implementation and additional training as needed. Each PLT also meets at least biweekly.

(Continued)

Table 2 (Continued)

Feature	Description	PLT Applications
Coherence (Desimone et al., 2002; Garet et al., 2001)	The activity promotes coherence in teachers' professional development by encouraging continued professional communication among teachers and by incorporating activities that align with standards and assessments, teachers' goals, and other school improvement efforts.	School leaders are expected to include the PLTs in their school improvement plans and ensure alignment or fit with other professional development activities for teachers. Some PLTs may incorporate aspects of curriculum alignment into their work.

groups, or schoolwide. Action research can foster a culture of collaborative problem solving and a team approach to school improvement when faculty members work together to conduct their inquiry (McTighe, 2008, p. 6). Participants examine their own practice systematically and carefully using research techniques. However, in contrast with traditional research, they are concerned with changing situations, not just interpreting them. Participants identify a problem, develop and implement a plan of action, collect and analyze data, and based on the results, plan for future action (Calhoun, 1994). Districtwide research can also be conducted, although it is more complex and uses more resources. Issues can be organizational, community based, performance based, or processes for decision making. A district may choose to address a problem common to several schools or only one (Ferrance, 2000).

Lesson Study

Lesson study was initially developed and used in Japan as a form of teacher research to engage teachers in systematically examining their own practice in order to increase effectiveness. Lesson study is a continuous professional development practice in which teachers collaboratively build pedagogical and content knowledge by planning, teaching, observing, and refining lessons. Working collaboratively, teachers establish goals, explore the content they are teaching, analyze instructional strategies, and examine student thinking and learning. Lesson study provides the structure for teachers to engage in research to investigate the impact their instructional decisions have on student understanding (for more information, see http://www.nwrel.org/lessonstudy/). In this model, teachers work collaboratively on a small number of lessons, planning, teaching, observing, and critiquing the lesson. Initially, they set a goal and develop a research question to guide their work. They design a detailed lesson plan, and one teaches it while the others observe. They then discuss their observations. The lesson may be revised and implemented by another teacher in a different classroom followed again by observation and discussion. The group will ultimately produce a report reflecting on their research question and learning from the process (Columbia University).

Critical Friends Group (CFG)

Critical Friends Group (CFG) was developed at the Annenberg Institute for School Reform in 1994 as an approach to professional development focused on teacher learning. In a CFG, several educators, usually between 8 and 12, meet monthly for about two hours with a goal of improving their practice through collaborative learning. They may discuss a specific article or book related to the group's interest. They use specific protocols to guide their discussion around topics such as examining student and teacher work, solving problems, setting goals, and peer observation. CFGs are expected to set norms for working together, listen actively, use guidelines for dialogue, and offer and receive both warm (supportive) and cool feedback (Nave, 2000).

Curry (2008) examined the choices of six CFGs and found, "Although CFGs enhanced teachers' collegial relationships, their awareness of research-based practices and reforms, their schoolwide knowledge, and their capacity to undertake instructional improvement, these professional communities offered an inevitably partial combination of supports for teacher professional development" (p. 734). The lack of influence on teachers' pedagogical content knowledge was the missing factor here. Curry suggests that in order to influence the academic gains schools are seeking, attention must be paid to regular reflection on ways to improve teacher practice as well as providing professional development in subject matter departments and interdisciplinary grade-level teams. This provides direction for all collaborative efforts in schools.

Looking at Student Work

Looking at student work in a teacher group can be a powerful vehicle for developing a teacher learning community. Teachers may examine the work of a single student or the response of several students to the same assignment. The focus is on student learning, not on teaching, and as such, provides some safety around collaboration. Using one of the many protocols to guide this process helps create a safe environment to present and discuss the student work with the idea that participating teachers learn from the activity (see http://www.lasw.org/ for additional information and protocols). Discussing student work encompasses ideas about improving instruction as well as assessing student learning (McLaughlin & Talbert, 2006).

Faculty Study Groups

Study groups may be small groups of teachers who decide to come together to focus on teaching and learning by reading, discussing, and sometimes conducting action research. A more intentional method, Whole-Faculty Study Groups (WFSG), is detailed by Murphy and Lick (2001). By definition, the entire faculty and sometimes teaching assistants participate in one of the smaller study groups across the school. Each group follows guidelines that include developing an action plan and keeping a log. The faculty analyzes student and school data to identify student needs and form groups based on those needs. Each group then determines what they will do to address the specific student need. "The goal of WFSGs is to focus the entire school faculty on creating, implementing, and integrating effective teaching and learning practices into school programs that will result in an increase in student learning and a decrease in negative behaviors of students, as reflected in related, relevant data sources" (p. 11).

Data Teams

The data team professional development process focuses on analyzing data, setting goals, implementing strategies, and assessing the effect to improve teaching and learning. As the name implies, data teams rely heavily on *data driven decision making*. They search out, organize and analyze data, prioritize needs, set and review annual goals, identify specify strategies to meet those goals, and determine performance measures or indicators to gauge results.

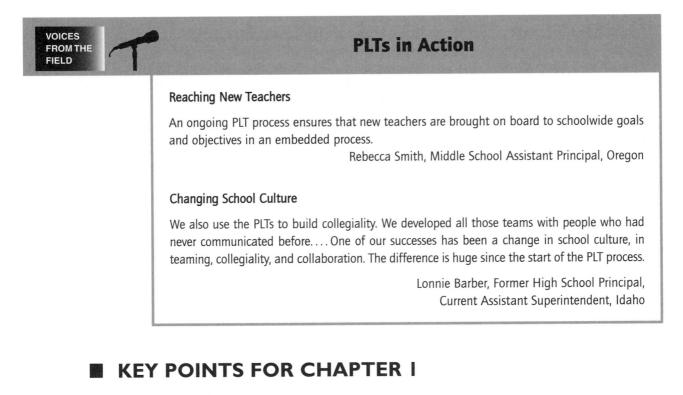

VOICES FROM THE FIELD

PLTs in Action

Reaching New Teachers

An ongoing PLT process ensures that new teachers are brought on board to schoolwide goals and objectives in an embedded process.

Rebecca Smith, Middle School Assistant Principal, Oregon

Changing School Culture

We also use the PLTs to build collegiality. We developed all those teams with people who had never communicated before.... One of our successes has been a change in school culture, in teaming, collegiality, and collaboration. The difference is huge since the start of the PLT process.

Lonnie Barber, Former High School Principal,
Current Assistant Superintendent, Idaho

■ KEY POINTS FOR CHAPTER 1

Understanding Professional Learning Teams

- PLTs follow an inquiry cycle with the goal of improving student achievement as they further develop teachers' skills.
- PLTs provide ongoing, job-embedded, team-based professional development that improves teaching quality.
- Through PLTs, teachers increase their collaboration skills as they integrate new teaching strategies into their repertoire.
- PLTs incorporate the six features of professional development linked by research to changes in teacher performance and student learning.
- PLTs are compatible and often complement other forms of professional development.

See Tool H-13 for the "Getting Started Roadmap," an abbreviated version of the contents of each chapter.

Understanding PLTs and Our School Context

LEADERSHIP TEAM DISCUSSION

- Why do we want to develop PLTs in our school?
- How will PLTs benefit our teachers and students?
- In what ways does our staff already work collaboratively?
- What needs to occur to encourage and support additional staff collaboration? How can we maximize the benefits of collaboration at our school?
- What kinds of professional development have our teachers experienced in the past? How do they align with the PLT process?
- Do we need more professional development? In what areas?

  - Collaboration skills
  - Using data to make decisions
  - Writing and honing questions to focus inquiry
  - Understanding and interpreting educational research
  - Classroom assessment and developing common assessments
  - Specific content areas

- What do we already have in place that enables and supports collaboration (e.g., common prep time for teachers)?
- How will our teachers access research information? Do we need to provide any research to them?
- Tool H-3 contains a sample agenda for the first workshop introducing teachers to PLTs.

Notes:

> *Through the process of improving lessons and sharing with colleagues the knowledge they acquire, something remarkable happens to teachers: They begin viewing themselves as true professionals. They see themselves as contributing to the knowledge base that defines the profession. And they see this as an integral part of what it means to be a teacher.*
>
> James W. Stigler &
> James Hiebert, 1999, pp. 126–127

2

Setting the Stage for Success

If moral purpose is job one, relationships are job two, as you can't get anywhere without them. In the past, if you asked someone in a successful enterprise what caused the success, the answer was "It's the people." But that's only partially true: it is actually the relationships that make the difference.

Michael Fullan, 2001b, p. 51

FOCUS OF THIS CHAPTER

- Are we ready to undertake Professional Learning Teams (PLTs) as a change effort?
- How can we understand change?
- What do we need to know about building relationships?
  - o Developing trust
  - o Creating a safe environment
  - o Working with conflict
- How do we create avenues of communication?
  - o Within the school
  - o Between the school staff and the district office
  - o With the teachers' union
  - o With parents and community members

■ READINESS FOR PLTs

Prior to embarking on the PLT process, school leaders need to allocate and use planning time—ideally at least six months—to prepare the entire staff to implement PLTs. Chapter 1 indicates that one-time or *drive-by* staff development experiences have a limited potential for changing practice and enhancing student achievement. On the other hand, PLTs used as an ongoing professional development process can positively change school climate and teachers' practice, along with student learning and achievement. This is most likely to take place when the PLT process becomes embedded in the ongoing work of teaching and learning within a school. Teachers need to meet regularly and collaborate with a consistent focus on improving student learning by changing classroom instruction. Chapters 2 and 3 can help prepare you and your staff to successfully undertake school change using PLTs.

Assess Current Conditions and Plan to Monitor Progress

It is important to understand the current conditions in the school that support the development of PLTs as well as provide potential challenges. Assessing what exists around staff perceptions can establish a baseline against which to measure progress as PLTs are implemented. The Northwest Regional Educational Laboratory (NWREL) developed two online surveys that can be used by school leaders to assist in assessing current conditions as well as to measure change annually.

The first survey, School Capacity for Continuous Improvement, helps assess school context and readiness for change. There is no charge to the school for completing the survey and receiving the school reports. After creating an account at http://www.nwrel.org/assessment/SchoolCapacity/setup.php, the entire staff can complete the survey online, and the school will receive a report for use in planning school reform and improvement efforts. There is no minimum score or cutoff point in the survey indicating a lack of readiness. However, this survey can provide an overview of school conditions and indicate areas needing attention. Survey questions are grouped under the following seven categories:

- Clear school direction (mission and vision)
- Shared facilitative leadership
- Staff collaboration
- Personal commitment by teachers
- Challenging curriculum and engaged student learning
- Communications with parents, community members, and business partners
- Meaningful involvement of parents, community members, and business partners

For more information on this survey, see Resource B or access www.nwrel.org/assessment/SchoolCapacity/about.php. Download the survey questions, interpretation guide, and sample reports to understand how the data will be reported.

Another online instrument, the Professional Learning Community survey, Resource C found at http://www.nwrel.org/csdi/services/plt/PLCSurvey/, measures the degree of professional community among teachers in a school across six facets demonstrated to have significant positive effects on student achievement:

- Organizational learning
- Collective responsibility
- Focus on student learning
- Reflective dialogue
- Staff collegiality and collaboration
- Deprivatized practice

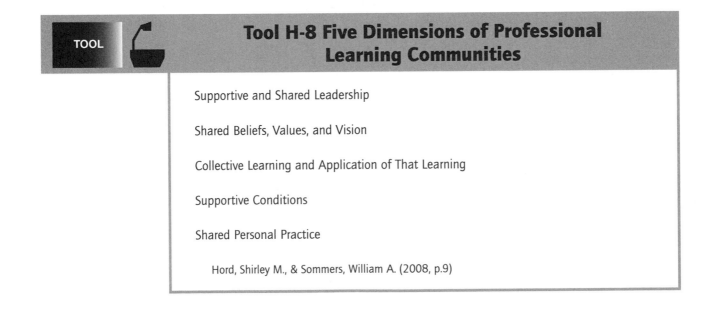

ACTION

Assessing Current Conditions

- Review and discuss the two surveys and their potential usefulness to the planning process.
- Decide if either of these meets your needs and provides information that is useful as you plan.
- Consider how you will share the results with teachers.
- You may use the results of both surveys to guide faculty discussion and learning about current strengths and needs.
- You may administer both surveys more than once to measure change in the staff over time.

The professional learning communities studied by Hall and Hord (2001) are aptly described as "communities of continuous inquiry and improvement" (Hord, 2004, p. 1). From the literature on professional learning communities, Hord compiled five attributes that describe the essential qualities or dimensions of professional learning communities. The following briefly describes these dimensions and Tool H-8 provides a master outlining them to stimulate discussion among team members.

TOOL

Tool H-8 Five Dimensions of Professional Learning Communities

Supportive and Shared Leadership

Shared Beliefs, Values, and Vision

Collective Learning and Application of That Learning

Supportive Conditions

Shared Personal Practice

Hord, Shirley M., & Sommers, William A. (2008, p.9)

- Shared and supportive leadership—power, authority, and decision making are shared by administrators and teachers. Leaders provide support for teachers working in PLTs.
- Shared beliefs, values, and vision—the staff is focused on improving student learning and strengthening this goal through their own learning. They understand the vision, including the underlying beliefs and values.
- Collective learning and application of that learning—staff determine *what* they need to learn and *how* to learn it to best meet identified student learning needs.
- Supportive conditions—structural factors include time and space for meeting, resources, and policies that support collaboration; relational factors support human and interpersonal development, openness, honesty, and attitudes of respect and caring.
- Shared personal practice—individuals make their teaching public as they give and receive feedback that supports both individual and organizational improvement (Hord, 2004; Hord & Sommers, 2008).

UNDERSTANDING CHANGE ■

School leaders need to acknowledge that developing PLTs as a way for teachers to work collaboratively and to focus on changing their own instruction may require a radical shift in attitudes, beliefs, and behavior for some people. The process of trying something new, sharing ideas and practice, and sometimes admitting the failure of a lesson or strategy can be challenging and threatening. To create supportive conditions requires a concerted effort to build and maintain trust.

It is important to understand and work with the change process. Responses to change are developmental, and teachers' concerns about the proposed change are real and require ongoing attention. The following information (adapted from Hord, Rutherford, Huling-Austin, & Hall, 1987) will assist school leaders in working with change at several stages.

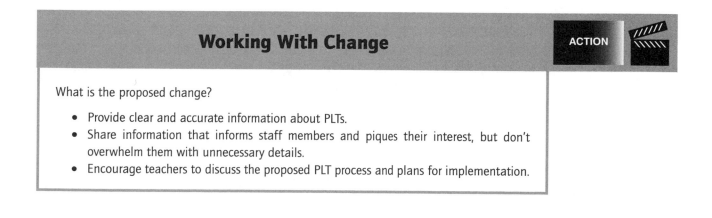

Working With Change   ACTION

What is the proposed change?

- Provide clear and accurate information about PLTs.
- Share information that informs staff members and piques their interest, but don't overwhelm them with unnecessary details.
- Encourage teachers to discuss the proposed PLT process and plans for implementation.

- Answer questions about PLTs and refer staff to relevant resources.
- Use multiple avenues to communicate about PLTs with individuals and small groups—verbal, written, and electronic (e-mail).
- Invite teachers from other schools implementing PLTs to speak with your staff and/or arrange visits to such schools.
- Help teachers see how PLTs relate to their current practices.
- Believe in and be enthusiastic about the change.

How will PLTs affect each individual?

- Acknowledge personal concerns—both teachers' and leaders' concerns.
- Encourage and reinforce each person's sense of efficacy through conversations and personal notes.
- Connect concerned teachers with others who will be supportive.
- Explain that PLTs will be implemented sequentially; establish realistic expectations.
- Encourage and support PLTs; maintain expectations while allowing each individual to move forward at his or her own pace.

How does each person find time to implement PLT processes and strategies?

- Answer the small, specific *how to* questions (refer to information on "finding time" in Resource D and tools H-9 and H-10 for ideas).
- Clarify the steps in the PLT process.
- Develop and share practical solutions to the logistical problems that underlie specific concerns.
- Assist teachers in sequencing activities and setting timelines.

How will PLTs affect our students?

- Share appropriate information about planned instructional changes with students.
- Increase opportunities for students to experience success.
- Develop and use ways for students to work collaboratively, extending the PLT process into classrooms.
- Celebrate success with students as well as teachers.

How do we discuss ideas and experience with others?

- Provide opportunities and tools for teachers to develop skills needed to work collaboratively.
- Assist collaborators in establishing reasonable expectations and guidelines for PLT efforts.
- Encourage individuals with strong collaborative skills to assist others.
- Acknowledge the efforts and participation of those who may not be natural collaborators.
- Model collaboration among leaders.

There is a significant body of literature on change in education. School leaders should become familiar with some of this literature and share ideas with the staff. The Suggested Reading section for this chapter contains a few recommended resources on change.

PLTs provide a structured approach to building a schoolwide professional learning community. PLTs have a greater chance of successful and ongoing implementation when school leaders establish structures that support collective learning, risk taking, and sharing personal practice. This includes building relationships within the school, developing and nurturing trust, creating avenues for communication, and working with conflict. While this chapter considers the relational aspects of PLTs, Chapter 3 looks at preparing for some of the more structural, practical needs of PLTs.

BUILDING RELATIONSHIPS ■

We form relationships with all members of the school community—colleagues, students, parents, and community representatives. The quality of these relationships makes a huge difference in the way a school and its teams function. Relationships happen simply through proximity. However, it is important to be intentional about building and sustaining healthy relationships. School leaders need to attend to the following:

- Build and maintain trust and create a safe environment for teachers to share openly.
- Explore ways to work with conflict as it comes up.
- Develop and use avenues for communicating with the entire school community, including parents and the district office.

Developing Trust

Building and nurturing trust in schools is an ongoing endeavor, one that is essential if teachers are to work collaboratively. While trust alone will not increase student achievement, it is vitally important for teachers to develop relationships and be able to talk with colleagues about sometimes thorny issues as they engage in collaborative problem solving focused on teaching and learning. This is central to a healthy, collegial school climate where people feel free to ask the necessary questions. PLT activities can assist with trust and relationship building. However, it is especially necessary for administrators and teacher leaders to initiate, model, and continually nurture trusting relationships among staff.

Drawing on years of longitudinal survey data—as well as in-depth interviews with principals, teachers, parents, and local community leaders in Chicago—Bryk and Schneider (2002) developed a thorough account of how effective social relationships or *relational trust* can serve as a prime resource for school improvement. In schools characterized by high relational trust, educators were more likely to experiment with new practices and work together to advance improvements. These schools were also more likely to demonstrate marked gains in student

> *A broad base of trust across a school community lubricates much of a school's day-to-day functioning and is a critical resource as local leaders embark on ambitious improvement plans.*
>
> Anthony S. Bryk & Barbara Schneider, 2002

learning. In contrast, schools with weak trust saw virtually no improvement in their reading or mathematics scores. The quality of social relationships strongly predicts positive student outcomes. A broad base of trust provides a crucial resource as educators embark on major school reforms. Bryk and Schneider (2002) observe, "social relationships at work in school communities comprise a fundamental feature of their operations. The nature of these social exchanges, and the local cultural features that shape them, condition the school's capacity to improve" (p. 5).

Relational trust serves as a resource for school improvement in four ways:

1. It helps moderate the sense of uncertainty and vulnerability experienced in the risk taking involved in change. Relational trust can serve as a catalyst for innovation.

2. Structural change efforts require intense collective decision making. Reform is likely to progress faster in high-trust contexts when participants are more able to coalesce around a plan of action and where relational trust facilitates public problem solving.

3. Relational trust increases the likelihood of broad-based, high-quality implementation of improvement efforts and helps coordinate meaningful collective action.

4. This trust constitutes a moral resource for school improvement; the normative understandings provide good reasons for engaging efforts that might seem irrational in a purely self-interested point of view—such as working longer hours or risking new practices that might fail (Bryk & Schneider, 2002, p. 5).

For principals to share leadership effectively, there must be a high level of trust among the administrator, other school leaders, and teachers. The following are suggested ways to build trust.

ACTION   **Steps to Building Trust**

- Maintain a focus on the common vision and values providing the basis for teachers' work. This means holding the students' best interests at the center of all decisions in the school. When making decisions, ask, "How does this serve our students?"
- Create and sustain supportive conditions for maintaining professional learning communities. Consider needs when developing a master schedule and assigning or moving classrooms.
- Increase communication with and between teachers, develop committees that have responsibility for major areas of school operation, and designate and protect specific time for teachers to study and learn together.
- Designate time for collective learning and model an appreciation for learning by constantly reading and making use of opportunities to learn from colleagues and experts. Discuss learning and how it applies to the school with teachers. (Fleming & Thompson, 2004, pp. 34–36)

Teachers, like students, want to feel safe in the school environment. This can mean different things to different people in different schools. In some schools, it is necessary to create sheer physical safety from violence and threats so that students and staff feel secure in coming to school. However, in the context of developing the PLT process, it is also essential to make it safe for teachers to try something new, to take a risk, to experiment with sometimes daring strategies, and occasionally to realize the strategies didn't work as envisioned. Thus, it becomes safe to admit a mistake, to learn from that experience, and to regroup and try something else. This requires leaders to work at trust building with staff as well as to communicate a sense of confidence in teachers: a belief that they can change their practice in ways that result in enhanced learning and achievement for their students. This parallels the need for teachers to express their belief in their students' abilities to change and learn increasingly complex concepts—in fact, to achieve at higher and higher levels.

This is particularly important as teachers are asked to share their practice and make their teaching public. Teaching has traditionally been a very private endeavor, one where the teacher closes the classroom door and shares very little with her colleagues. However, teachers in successful schools value and participate in norms of collegiality and continuous improvement, indicating that *working together* to improve teaching has a positive effect on student learning (Little, 1982, 2002).

Build Relationships With Staff and Students

VOICES FROM THE FIELD

Understand and deal with the fact that the work is draining—part physical, part emotional—working in schools with kids and adults. Relationships are important. With students in poverty and minority students, until those relationships are built, no learning will take place. In the same way, not much happens until there is a trusting relationship with the staff. You have to build confidence and trust—then better things will happen. Make sure the teachers believe you have confidence in them. Your actions will show this—stand behind them. Sometimes allow them to make a mistake and learn from it.

Darrel Burbank, Retired Elementary Principal, Idaho

At the heart of creating a safe environment is relationship building. Working and learning together in teams is a complex process that requires individuals to understand themselves. They must also understand their beliefs, thoughts, and motives, as well as those of other group members (Wald & Castleberry, 1999). Teamwork melds individual interests into a collective shared journey. It also requires group agreements and understandings that create bonds of trust, belonging, and purposefulness. These complexities are more easily addressed when the group takes the time to establish the groundwork for building relationships and to define the agreements or *norms* for working with one another (Johnson & Johnson, 1994; Katzenbach & Smith, 1999; Maeroff, 1993; Murphy & Lick, 1998; Schmuck & Runkel, 1994; Senge, Kleiner, Roberts, Ross, & Smith, 1994). Those *working agreements* should be revisited and revised from time to time to ensure they fit for the team members' needs. Teams may change members at the beginning of a new school year and it is important to establish working conditions that support the new team, allowing each teacher to have a voice.

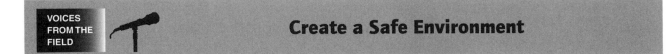

| VOICES FROM THE FIELD | **Create a Safe Environment** |

In order to build a safe environment, go to teachers on their own turf—almost like a doctor making rounds. Try to walk through every room every morning to say hello. This helps establish an atmosphere where teachers feel safe. They will then be more likely to bring up their issues and concerns when they find that you are approachable. Realize that some teachers may find it more difficult to meet in your office—going through the secretary, entering your space, and closing the door. The principal is sitting behind a desk in his or her big office, and the only place for the teacher is on the other side of the desk. You have to create open space for the teacher. When meeting in your office, get out from behind that desk—use a table for those meetings.

Darrel Burbank, Retired Elementary Principal, Idaho

Working With Conflict

Some level of conflict is inevitable in any group, particularly one with an emphasis on changing the status quo. When teachers collaborate, they may run headlong into disagreements over professional beliefs and practices. Their norms of privacy, independence, and professional autonomy may be challenged (Achinstein, 2002b). Thus, conflict may occur in schools, particularly during the reform process. Healthy organizations use conflict as an opportunity to grow while exploring divergent points of view. As Hirsh (2003) points out, "the more ambitious the change that is sought, the more problems. In order to accomplish significant change, schools must be able to successfully manage their problems."

> *When teachers work together in small groups and in a truly collaborative sense, relationships and school climate changes. Teachers tell me that they can speak up in their grade-level meetings but feel intimidated in whole-staff meetings. The small groups support a deeper level of self-reflection.*
>
> Timothy Oberg, Elementary Principal, Gresham, Oregon

PLTs are intentionally kept small with only four to six members in a team: The limited size ensures that everyone participates fully in the process. It also provides enough individual voices to encourage diverse opinions and thoughts. Keeping teams small has the added benefit of making it easier to resolve the inevitable conflicts and disagreements.

PLTs delve deeply into curriculum and pedagogy, striving to understand what produces real learning in students. Team members labor intensively to understand what is working or not working in the classroom and why they are getting those results. They then extend, adapt, or abandon specific practices as needed. Some teachers have developed a comfortable routine as a survival mechanism during their years of teaching.

PLTs assist them in "learning from experience and turning problems into possibilities for change rather than falling back on old patterns" (Richardson & Placier, 2001, p. 937). Such in-depth reflection and analysis may threaten familiar foundations and can provoke discomfort, fear, and sometimes anger. It is important to allow and acknowledge these feelings so they do not undermine the cohesion and work of the team.

What school leaders do to prepare for and work with conflict is an important aspect of supporting PLTs in a school. For many people, conflict can be disconcerting. Yet acknowledging and working with conflict can help promote individual and organizational learning and growth. Debate and controversy can be positive elements in a school's culture when individuals consciously work to maintain a constructive level of conflict and debate while keeping a respectful attitude (Uline, Tschannen-Moran, & Perez, 2003). "Conflict, it turns out, offers a context for inquiry, organizational learning, and change. As colleagues air differences, build understanding across perspectives, and see changes enhanced by divergent thinking, conflict becomes constructive for the community and school" (Achinstein, 2002a, p. 3).

Viewing conflict as an opportunity for growth—a chance to explore differences and learn from and about each other—can dispel fear and guard against avoidance. In this way, conflict can be reframed as positive and play an important part in the development of healthy work relationships (Wilmot & Hocker, 2001). The Wilmot-Hocker Conflict Assessment Guide contains a series of questions that may be used to bring specific aspects of a conflict into focus by providing essential information about the conflict that might otherwise remain unknown (Wilmot & Hocker, 2001, pp. 204–207). Rather than trying to head off conflict at every turn, it is important to acknowledge the potential and use the opportunity to learn and grow together. There are many models for conflict resolution, including one by Stephanie Hirsh (2003) and the National Staff Development Council. See Resource E for specifics of that model.

Acknowledge Conflict

ACTION

It is recommended that leaders discuss and prepare for conflict. Some of the following ideas may be used to guide discussion:

- Assess the options, choose a conflict resolution model, and train staff in its use prior to an actual conflict.
- Find out if some staff members already use a specific conflict resolution model, and explore the potential for using this model.
- Consider using a single model schoolwide. It can provide a common language that everyone understands and an accessible way to work with other areas of conflict. However, some teams may want to choose or develop their own model.

- Develop some common and believable scenarios for teams to practice using the model. (See Resource F for some suggested scenarios. To conduct this activity with staff, it may be more successful to develop scenarios that fit you own specific school context.)

Activity: Unspoken Issues

1. Lead an open discussion on the following questions:
   - There is an unwritten taboo around discussing some issues. What are some of the issues that we avoid and *never* discuss?
   - Why do we not confront those particular issues?
   - What are the risks and costs of discussing these issues?
   - What actions can we take to deal with these issues?

2. Then ask team members to individually reflect on any issues that are getting in the way of group work, either in the school as a whole, or within their own team. Have each person fill out an anonymous 3x5 card with their concerns and give it to the facilitator.

3. Review responses and share one that might be most easily addressed. Facilitate a group resolution of the issue. Write the concern and resolution on chart paper for all to see.

4. When appropriate, move on to more difficult issues.

■ CREATING AVENUES OF COMMUNICATION

The PLT planning process provides an opportune time to think about how communication occurs within the school; between the school, parents, and community; with other schools; and with the district office. It is highly important to share information about change efforts up front with others in the school community in order to develop buy-in and anticipate some of the challenges that may occur during implementation. Two commonly used ways to communicate are newsletters and e-mail notices.

> *Now we all respect each other's opinions. Before, people would leave in the middle of meetings if there was conflict.*
>
> Teacher in PLT

However, the most effective communication is often face-to-face sharing. Involving the leadership team in planning for implementation is an important but insufficient level of communication prior to PLT implementation. Information needs to be shared with the wider school community, including these stakeholders:

- The entire school staff, both classified employees and teachers
- The district office and school board
- The teachers' union
- Parents and the community

Informing the School Staff

Teachers will be responsible for implementing PLTs and infusing the agreed upon strategies into their daily work. They are closest to the action in classrooms and the primary movers in the change process in any school. Teacher representatives should be included in the planning committee. Their understanding and buy-in to the process are essential for success. Thus, they must be kept respectfully in the information loop during the planning process. Involving a large staff in every aspect of planning is unwieldy and nearly impossible. Yet we suggest providing regular updates to the entire staff so there are no surprises. Teachers themselves may be the best emissaries to keep staff informed. We also recommend involving the entire staff in making important decisions that affect their work and lives.

An ancillary step is to listen to the naysayer to understand and possibly circumvent some potential problems during implementation. On every teaching staff, you will likely find three types of participants: (1) some teachers will readily embrace change efforts, (2) some will adopt a "wait and see" stance, and (3) a few will resist the change, either openly or covertly. Those resisters may have important information to consider during both planning and implementation. When possible, an effective method of involving and informing some of the resisters is to send them to visit a school that is successfully implementing the PLT process. (For additional suggestions on dealing with the resisters, see Chapter 5.)

The classified staff is sometimes more closely connected than teachers are to the community at large and to parents in particular. They need to be kept informed about proposed changes, particularly since scheduling changes may affect their workday at times. In addition, they often need to respond to informal questions from parents and other community members. In some schools, paraprofessionals are also more directly representative of the community. They may be the only staff members who speak the same language as some of the parents. Another early decision to be discussed in planning PLTs is whether teams will include paraprofessionals.

> I think you have to disseminate to teachers on one hand and to superintendents, central office folks, and principals on the other. Those in the latter category are the agents for changing the structure of the workplace. Central office folks need to be deeply involved in the process and need to create structures that small teams of teachers and most schools cannot make without their help.
>
> Bruce Joyce, 2004, p. 81

Keys to Communicating   ACTION

Consider ways to do the following:

- Keep the staff informed during the planning process.
- Plan systematic ways to share information—e-mail, newsletters, regular updates at staff and parent meetings.
- Include the classified staff in the information loop.
- Involve staff in making important decisions that affect their work.
- Provide for a feedback loop to continue to gather staff and community input.
- Listen to the naysayer; seek out the resisters; ask and prepare to listen with an open mind to their objections.

■ KEY POINTS FOR CHAPTER 2

- Time spent planning and preparing prior to developing PLTs contributes to successful implementation.
- Assessing staff's readiness can assist in understanding the current school climate as well as anticipate areas requiring immediate and long-term attention.
- Learning about and working with change may ease the transition.
- Being intentional about building relationships among staff members and with important stakeholders is very important.
- Trust is a central component of relationship building and a necessary condition for school change efforts.
- Conflict will come up; anticipating and preparing for it helps.
- Intentionally building avenues for communication and keeping important stakeholders informed can support change efforts.

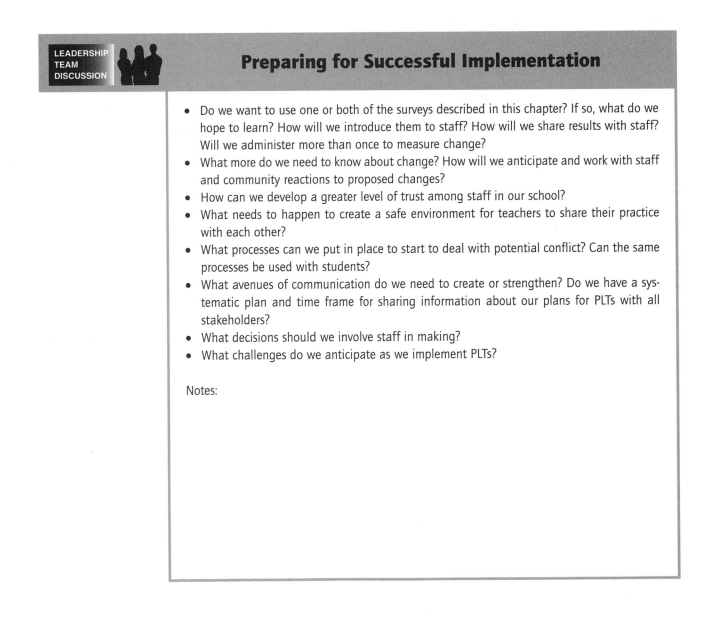

LEADERSHIP TEAM DISCUSSION

Preparing for Successful Implementation

- Do we want to use one or both of the surveys described in this chapter? If so, what do we hope to learn? How will we introduce them to staff? How will we share results with staff? Will we administer more than once to measure change?
- What more do we need to know about change? How will we anticipate and work with staff and community reactions to proposed changes?
- How can we develop a greater level of trust among staff in our school?
- What needs to happen to create a safe environment for teachers to share their practice with each other?
- What processes can we put in place to start to deal with potential conflict? Can the same processes be used with students?
- What avenues of communication do we need to create or strengthen? Do we have a systematic plan and time frame for sharing information about our plans for PLTs with all stakeholders?
- What decisions should we involve staff in making?
- What challenges do we anticipate as we implement PLTs?

Notes:

Laying the Foundation Within the School Community

With stubborn resolve and ingenuity, every school creates or sets aside time needed for staff to plan programs, exchange ideas, and reflect together about instruction, student needs, and teacher growth. This vital resource of time is indispensable for all aspects of the culture shift [to a professional learning community] we've examined so far.

WestEd, 2000, p. 35

FOCUS OF THIS CHAPTER

- Where do we need to advocate for PLTs?
- Do we need to align PLT efforts with overall school improvement goals?
- What structures support PLTs?

  o Developing the leadership team
  o Allocating time for PLTs to meet

- What do teams do with data?
- How do we ensure accountability?
- What additional resources might be needed?

■ ADVOCATING FOR PLTs WITH IMPORTANT STAKEHOLDERS

In addition to keeping teachers and classified staff in the information loop, informing other stakeholders about the proposed change and potential value for students and teachers can help build much needed support.

The District Office and School Board

It is important to communicate with the district office about the nature, purpose, and extent of PLT work in your school. Research indicates that district support is central to lasting change that affects powerful teaching and learning in schools (Bodilly & Berends, 1999; McLaughlin & Talbert, 2003). "The district administrator is the single most important individual for setting the expectation and tone of the pattern of change within the local district" (Fullan, 1991, p. 11). This underscores the importance of keeping the district office well informed about the PLT goals and processes as the school works to transform teaching and learning. District and sometimes school board approval will be necessary for changing school schedules to accommodate collaborative work time for teachers. In addition, district and board support—or lack of it—can often make or break change efforts. Developing fluency with the PLT process helps school leaders as they reach out to the district and community to build understanding and necessary support as the school works to enhance student learning. Some of the tools found in Resource H may be used in presentations about PLTs. Also, information gained from surveys (Resources B and C) may be used to justify the need for professional development as a school or district shifts to implementing PLTs.

ACTION

Making Your Case

The Small Schools Project provides a set of tips to help you organize and prepare a school board presentation to request collaboration time. The advice is also useful when talking to district administrators as well as parent groups. Among the project's suggestions are the following:

- Be clear about the support you are asking for.
- What is the proposed change?
- What is the underlying rationale (see Chapter 1)?
- What is the intended outcome?
- Describe what collaboration means and what teachers will be doing during that time.
- Show how this time translates to student learning.

Additional suggestions are available on the Small Schools Project Web site at www.smallschoolsproject.org/PDFS/asking_board_for_collab_time.pdf.

Involving the Teachers' Union

In the literature, teachers' unions are rarely viewed as collaborative players. However, that is not necessarily the case. In the Spokane (Washington) School District, the teachers' union was a key player, working with the school board and district administration to develop a restructuring plan. This plan included a successful districtwide effort to create professional learning communities with a central and successful focus on increasing student achievement (Sather, 2004). Unions also worked collaboratively with school districts in Boston, New York, and Columbus, Ohio, to redesign high schools into smaller learning communities (Milliken, Ross, Pecheone, & Darling-Hammond, 2006).

Rather than viewing unions as hindering the process, it is crucial to inform and bring them in as partners. They need to be involved in discussions and planning as early as possible. Developing a good working relationship with the union and eliciting its understanding and support can be key to successful implementation of PLTs.

Involve the Union

VOICES FROM THE FIELD

Involving the education association/union in planning from the beginning can help with contractual agreements, planning for release time, assistance in motivating staff members, communicating the relevance to student learning, and NCLB requirements, among other things.

Erin McGary-Hamilton, Former K–8 Principal, Education Northwest Staff Member

---

Informing Parents and Community Members

Parents need to be kept in the loop during PLT planning and implementation. Planning that involves schedule changes—such as periodic late starts or early dismissal times—can affect day-care arrangements as well as parents' schedules in dropping off or picking up their children. Some parents may object to their adolescent children being released early without adequate supervision. This means that the principal and leadership team need to fully understand and be able to explain the PLT process and to justify the time allotted for teachers to learn and work together. The leadership team may be called on more than once to provide a compelling rationale for this form of professional development.

Community support for schools does make a difference, especially when undertaking significant changes and reforms. The appropriate district and school administrators may fully believe in the PLT process and throw their wholehearted support behind them. However, administrators have a way of moving or being moved around. Support can evaporate overnight when a new administrator arrives with his or her own priorities and beliefs about the most effective school improvement. Under this circumstance, community support for an ongoing initiative can be instrumental in securing its continuation. (See Chapter 4 for additional information about sustaining leadership.)

■ ALIGNING WITH SCHOOL GOALS

Professional development needs to be part of a long-term plan focused on improving student learning. "Change in professional practice is difficult and requires systematic support to implement and sustain it over time" (Wood & Thompson, 1993, p. 55). There is empirical support from research "for the contention that professional development that emphasizes content knowledge, active learning, and coherence leads to teachers reporting enhanced knowledge and skill and changes in teaching practices" (Garet, Birman, Porter, Desimone, & Herman with Yoon, 1999, p. 11).

> *Self-reflection is an important piece, helping to avoid "random acts of improvement." Teachers and teams need to ask questions:*
>
> *What is our achievement goal with this activity at this time?*
>
> *Is the activity aligned with where we want to go?*
>
> *Is it aligned with our school and grade level goals?*
>
> *What do we want our students to look like at the end of this activity?*
>
> Timothy Oberg, Elementary
> Principal, Gresham, Oregon

PLTs need to be part of a coherent plan for improving the success of all students. Coherence means that professional learning is set within a larger school-improvement effort that takes place over multiple years, focuses on specific goals tied to student learning, and is included in the school's written plan. Coherence in ongoing professional development is achieved when it builds upon previous efforts, promotes ongoing communication and interaction with colleagues, is aligned with school goals and standards, and is tied to student learning (Garet et al., 1999). Incorporating the PLT process into individual teacher professional growth plans reinforces this alignment.

Integrating professional development into the larger picture of comprehensive school improvement is critical (Cibulka & Nakayama, 2000; Garet, Porter, Desimone, Birman, & Yoon, 2001; Hawley & Valli, 1999; King & Newmann, 2000; Lewis, 2000; Smylie, Allensworth, Greenberg, Harris, & Luppescu, 2001; Wood & Thompson, 1993). The importance of professional learning reaches a higher level when linked to the larger, comprehensive, and systemic schoolwide effort connected to state standards.

Teachers need to understand and keep the school improvement plan in mind when examining data. While focus questions should be developed by each PLT in relation to identified needs that emerge in scrutinizing data, they should also connect to the school improvement plan. We assume that data were used when developing this plan. If current needs are not addressed in the plan and more pressing needs have been identified, revisions to the plan may be in order.

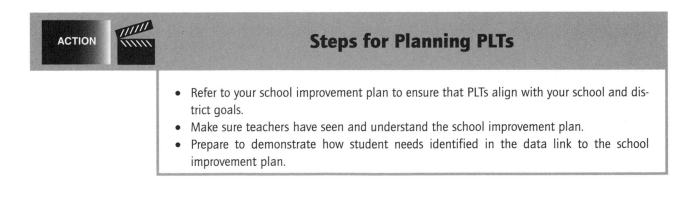

ACTION **Steps for Planning PLTs**

- Refer to your school improvement plan to ensure that PLTs align with your school and district goals.
- Make sure teachers have seen and understand the school improvement plan.
- Prepare to demonstrate how student needs identified in the data link to the school improvement plan.

- Acknowledge and take into account other professional development that teachers have experienced.
- Incorporate PLT implementation into teachers' professional growth plans.

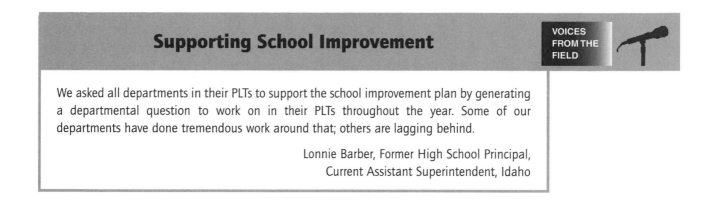

Supporting School Improvement

VOICES FROM THE FIELD

We asked all departments in their PLTs to support the school improvement plan by generating a departmental question to work on in their PLTs throughout the year. Some of our departments have done tremendous work around that; others are lagging behind.

Lonnie Barber, Former High School Principal,
Current Assistant Superintendent, Idaho

STRUCTURES FOR WORKING COLLABORATIVELY ■

It is important to think about and begin to put in place structures that will support the successful implementation of PLTs. The following structures and the way they are developed and put to use will influence school climate and successful PLT implementation:

- Working with a leadership team
- Allocating time for PLTs to be trained and meet together
- Ensuring access to current data
- Establishing accountability

The Leadership Team

Shared leadership structures include the leadership team, school improvement team, school site council, and faculty council, among others. Shared leadership of necessity includes shared decision making. Supporting teacher leadership means providing the structures, time, and distribution of work that allow teachers to lead. It also means providing time within the school day or extra pay for fulfilling leadership duties. When these conditions are missing, it is "difficult for teacher leaders to negotiate reasonable personal and professional lives" (Bartlett, 2001, in Lieberman & Miller, 2004, p. 19).

Many schools already have a leadership team in place. That team may be spearheading the school improvement process or convening to address issues such as discipline, low achievement, school restructuring, or meeting district and state initiatives. Involving teacher leaders in planning for PLT implementation helps develop necessary buy-in to the process and may be instrumental in eliciting staff ownership. Teacher leaders can effectively communicate important information about PLTs to their colleagues. They may be better able than administrators to anticipate challenges and effectively work to overcome them.

During the past three decades, "a large and growing volume of research repeatedly finds that, when principals empower their staffs by sharing leadership and decision making authority with them, everyone benefits, including students" (Cotton, 2003, p. 21). If a school has not yet developed a leadership team, embarking on planning for PLTs can be an opportune time to form such a team since PLTs, in turn, help build teacher leadership. When forming teams, it is important to build in diversity: take into account potential team members' backgrounds, culture and ethnicity, experience, gender, and views on education. In addition to including current teacher leaders and the union representative, consider which teachers are respected and trusted by their colleagues and communicate well with them.

When developing a leadership team, check for state and district guidelines. The composition of some teams is often specified. For instance, some states require parent participation on school improvement teams or school site councils.

There are several ways to develop a leadership team, each with its own set of benefits and challenges:

- Simply ask for volunteers. This may or may not prompt the most qualified individuals to indicate their interest.
- Appoint teachers who, in the administrator's opinion, have leadership potential. This may result in a strong working team but can also leave the principal open to criticism about playing favorites.
- Ask the group of teachers being represented to elect members to the team. This can work as long as it is not simply a popularity contest.
- Post a job description and open the position to all applicants. This process can take longer but may also result in a stronger team made up of motivated individuals.

Allocating Time for Professional Learning

Prior to beginning the PLT work, the administrator(s) and leadership team will need to establish dedicated time for PLTs to meet for the entire school year. Time is always a precious commodity in schools. However, it is critical to the success of PLTs to carve out time for professional learning during the planning phase. "Those wanting to create and sustain PLCs in their schools and districts must be committed to long-term and in-depth change, and that requires time" (Hord, 2004, p. 70).

Teachers need regularly scheduled time to meet together in their teams to accomplish their agreed upon work. Ideally, they meet for at least 90 minutes twice a month or 60 minutes weekly. It is important that this time is protected to ensure that PLT members have the time to be successful in changing their practices. If PLT time is frequently co-opted for other uses, the work of the teams will be diluted in ways that diminish intended outcomes. Meeting more frequently is desirable: limiting time to one long monthly meeting interrupts the flow of team thinking and may make it challenging for teachers to focus on group efforts to improve student learning. Quality team time requires a commitment by both administrators and teachers.

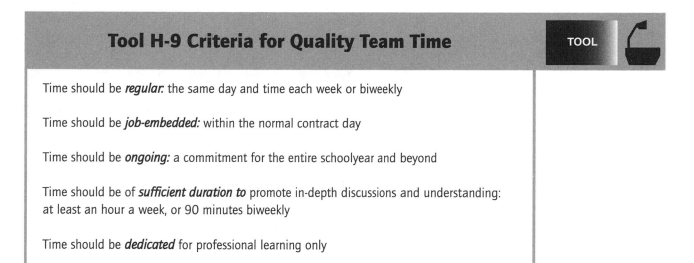

Tool H-9 Criteria for Quality Team Time　　TOOL

Time should be *regular:* the same day and time each week or biweekly

Time should be *job-embedded:* within the normal contract day

Time should be *ongoing:* a commitment for the entire schoolyear and beyond

Time should be of **sufficient duration to** promote in-depth discussions and understanding: at least an hour a week, or 90 minutes biweekly

Time should be *dedicated* for professional learning only

The time created for professional collaboration and learning must be ongoing and embedded within teachers' regular schedules. Developing new procedures for improvement in schools requires working with staff for a period of time so they increasingly come to understand, modify, become skilled in, and believe in the effectiveness of the new approach to change (Fullan, 1991, p. 213). A deep understanding of new practices requires a significant commitment by school leaders to allocate and protect adequate time, more than simply using occasional inservice days. One-day workshops or week-long institutes can initiate change, but further learning and collaboration are necessary to sustain change over time (Daniels, Bizar, & Zemelman, 2001, p. 243).

Redesigning the school schedule to provide increased collegial learning and planning time for teachers requires revising our concept about what constitutes the work of teachers. "Research and development time is necessary if teachers are to be effective while they are with students. Legitimate teacher work time is not limited to student contact time" (Katzenmeyer & Moller, 1996, p. 67). Most teachers understand that seat time doesn't guarantee student learning, yet some believe teaching time can eventually guarantee accomplished teaching (NCTAF, 1996). Ironically, teachers often feel guilty and resist taking time away from their students for their own learning (Maeroff, 1993). "Change in education will be held back as long as the notion persists" with teachers, as well as other educational stakeholders, "that teachers are at work only when they are in their classrooms instructing children" (p. 121). The leadership team may need to develop a plan to support altering school schedules for the public—community members as well as parents.

However, time for teachers to improve their own learning must not come at the expense of the amount of time students spend learning. The benefits to student achievement through improving the quality of instruction should not be counterbalanced by reducing its quantity. We cannot improve student achievement "with the amount of time now available and the way we now use it. Limited time will frustrate our aspirations. Misuse of time will undermine our best efforts" (National Education Commission on Time and Learning, 1994,

2005, p. 9). The six-hour school day and 180-day school year are the "unacknowledged design flaw in American education" and a "foundation of sand" for our educational system (p. 8). Responding to low student achievement by simply increasing teacher contact time "is flawed, even when considered from the perspective of the factory model. If an assembly line were producing defective products, an appropriate response would be to examine the process and improve it, not run the line an extra hour each day or an extra month each year" (DuFour & Eaker, 1998, p. 122). The 2005 revision of *Prisoners of Time,* the 1994 report by the National Education Commission on Time and Learning, maintains the conclusion that "both learners and teachers need more time, not to do more of the same, but to use all time in new, different, and better ways. The key to liberating learning lies in unlocking time" (p. 8).

The following options help school leaders envision the possibilities for allocating precious time to professional learning. The success of these strategies depends on considerable planning, learning, and discussion before their implementation. Resource D contains descriptive examples of ways that some schools have created additional time for teacher learning and collaboration. Also, Tools H-9 and H-10 include reproducible masters for "Criteria for Quality Team Time" and "Finding Time for Collaboration."

> *Traditional, inflexible scheduling is based on administrative and institutional needs. New, more flexible scheduling patterns are based on pedagogical practice, the educational needs of students, and the professional needs of teachers.*
>
> Gary D. Watts & Shari Castle, 1993, p. 307

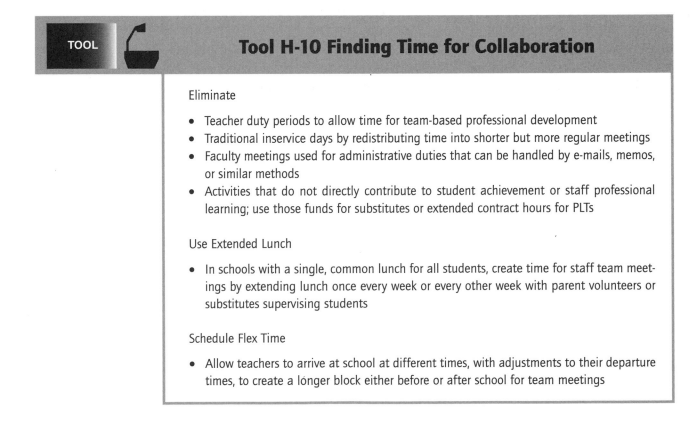

TOOL

Tool H-10 Finding Time for Collaboration

Eliminate

- Teacher duty periods to allow time for team-based professional development
- Traditional inservice days by redistributing time into shorter but more regular meetings
- Faculty meetings used for administrative duties that can be handled by e-mails, memos, or similar methods
- Activities that do not directly contribute to student achievement or staff professional learning; use those funds for substitutes or extended contract hours for PLTs

Use Extended Lunch

- In schools with a single, common lunch for all students, create time for staff team meetings by extending lunch once every week or every other week with parent volunteers or substitutes supervising students

Schedule Flex Time

- Allow teachers to arrive at school at different times, with adjustments to their departure times, to create a longer block either before or after school for team meetings

Hire Substitute Teachers or Administrative Substitutes

- Release teams of teachers during the workday for meetings, using a *regular team of substitutes to help ensure continuity in the classrooms*
- Use administrators as substitutes for some of the teachers, allowing them to get to know students in a different context and to showcase curricular and instructional strategies

Regularly Schedule Early Dismissal or Late Arrival for Students

- Lengthen some school days to allow more time on other days for team meetings
- Use time during some school days for students to engage in service learning or offer school-to-work internships to students

Establish Special Studies Day or Time

- Create a block or blocks of time throughout a week for all the students of one team of teachers to meet with specialists in the building, freeing that team to work together

Create a Four-Day Student Week

- Lengthen each school day to maintain student-teacher contact time and to enable staff to have one full day a week to meet in teams

Use Block and Modified-Block Schedules

- Create block schedules to provide longer periods of time for in-depth student and staff learning as teachers adopt instructional strategies suited to longer classes

Identify Viable Options for Finding Time   ACTION

Schedule time for the leadership team to discuss the need and identify realistic ways to provide and protect time for teachers to meet. The following suggestions may help the team (or entire staff) work with this issue:

- Take each of the main categories listed on "Finding Time for Collaboration" (Tool H-10). You may include expanded information and examples contained in Resource D. Divide participants into smaller groups and assign one or two categories per group.
- Have each group brainstorm and list pros and cons of the suggestions described in their category.
- Regroup, share ideas, and rank order suggestions from most likely to least likely choices for your specific school and district context.
- Begin planning steps to move forward on providing time for collaborative professional learning for teachers. Remember that asking the school board to change the school calendar or class schedule may require significant lead time.
- Plan when and how you inform the staff, parents, and other community members about schedule changes.

■ PROVIDING AND USING DATA

Schools use data for a variety of purposes:

- To guide their journey of improving teaching and learning
- To prioritize where improvements most urgently need to be made
- To gain relevant information as a basis for making effective instructional decisions
- To determine how well the school, one program, a group of teachers (such as a grade level), or single teachers are meeting the learning needs of students
- To set goals and evaluate progress toward achieving those goals
- To allocate resources where they are most needed
- To ensure quality implementation of new programs, ideas, or practices and to document the strengths and weaknesses of current ones
- To assess effectiveness of new programs and practices
- To furnish concrete evidence of achievements as a basis for celebration

PLTs use data at three important times in the process. First, they use school-wide achievement data to begin to pinpoint student learning needs. They may establish teams based on teacher self-selection according to teachers' interests and desire to tackle specific areas. Next, each team digs deeper into the data, using its findings to develop one or two focus questions that guide the work. To gain a more complete picture of student needs, teams may request or search out additional data at this time. Finally, teams develop ways to assess student learning related to their specific focus and use that data to monitor ongoing progress. While the annual test data serve as a starting point, teams are encouraged to use more specific measures, develop common assessments and other ways to gauge incremental progress, and make adjustments to teaching strategies when appropriate.

Making Data Accessible for Teachers

The challenge for leaders is to provide data in a variety of user-friendly formats—bar graphs, line graphs, and scatter plots—and to train teachers to systematically examine and use the information. The preliminary legwork to make sure data are accessible is crucial. Some districts use a data warehouse and then train teachers how to access that information. Other districts have central office staff dedicated to preparing data for each school. Some schools assign specific staff members to guide this process and serve as a data team. In any case, ensuring that data and training are available is central to the school improvement process.

State and district test scores provide a particular set of data; that information needs to be disaggregated by grade level, ethnicity, gender, economic status, language ability, and special programs. It is more useful if these scores include strand information so teachers can identify student learning needs in terms of specific skills that will require attention. For example, knowing that certain grade levels are weak in reading comprehension is much more useful if that information also provides a way to identify areas such as *making inferences* or *identifying the main idea and supporting details*. In addition, teachers are most interested in data on *their own* students. Make sure the data can be organized to provide this level of specificity. Some teachers choose to focus on a particular group of students. For example, they might focus on the 30 percent of their students scoring the lowest in a specific area. Thus, having the ability to manipulate the data to access and track with this type of information is beneficial.

Access to other kinds of assessments can be equally important. For example, attendance patterns, disciplinary referrals, course enrollment and completion, and grading patterns help round out the picture of school and class context. In addition, it is especially useful for a team to have access to cohort-trend data— three or more years of data on the same group of students. They can look for patterns, strengths, and needs that their current group of students may carry with them from grade to grade. School climate information can also reveal some areas needing attention. While climate is a significant component of the learning environment, it is important not to let climate issues overtake the inquiry into what is happening in classrooms in terms of student learning.

One note on disaggregating by race: Beware of overgeneralization. For example, *Asian* is a standard response in collecting demographic data, but the values, beliefs, and behavioral norms of different Asian cultures vary widely. These cultural differences have led to different collective experiences in immigrant groups and influence the relative success of each in adjusting to life in the United States and to our educational system. Korean students may have needs that are very different from Vietnamese students, and such needs may disappear under an aggregate *Asian* data. This principle also holds true for Hispanic, Middle Eastern, African American, and Eastern European cultures, among others.

Providing Training to Interpret Data

Data can provide a daunting challenge for some individuals. Giving teachers a huge set of test scores—even in multiple formats—without some training in interpretation and analysis can provoke *downshifting*. Downshifting occurs when an individual perceives an experience as threatening. This is "accompanied by a sense of helplessness and lack of self-efficacy . . . . Downshifting, then, appears to affect many higher order cognitive functions of the brain and thus can prevent us from learning and generating solutions for new problems" (Caine & Caine, 1994, pp. 69–70). This holds true for teachers as well as students. Thus, during planning for PLTs, prepare to assess teachers' needs for training to interpret and use data and ensure these needs will be met. As teachers become more adept at using data, they can be encouraged to request additional types of data to inform their practice.

> *The correlation between schools where the staff uses data and those not using data is night and day. Learning-focused conversations around data are invaluable in guiding school change that positively affects student achievement.*
>
> Joe Kinney, Former Assessment
> Director, Spokane, Washington

Analyzing Data

An entire school staff, as well as the individual PLT, engages in data analysis to accomplish two purposes: to set student and staff learning goals and to monitor progress toward those goals. Both goal setting and monitoring are more effective when data analysis and interpretation occur through the lens of the school's own context. Improving student learning should be the ultimate focus of this work.

Analyzing data for the purpose of either setting goals or monitoring progress is best handled by the people who are responsible for meeting those goals—namely, the teachers themselves. A leadership team or committee can ensure productive use of staff time by facilitating data collection and organizing the information into user-friendly displays to share with teachers. Creating meaning from the displays then becomes a collective task for the entire teaching staff.

When examining data, it is useful to use both year-to-year and cohort analysis. Year-to-year analysis compares the current year's data to the previous year and helps us understand the consistent impact of teaching and curriculum practices. If, for example, students overall do better in certain content areas and less well in others for several years, this tells us how well the curriculum and instructional techniques work and indicates areas of need. Cohort analysis can be a more reliable indicator of classroom effectiveness. By comparing students' results in one year to the same students' results in the next year, we can understand the impact of curriculum and teaching on that group. This type of analysis controls for the impact of mobility and absenteeism (Reeves, 2003).

> *We felt that evidence from data indicated the work of PLTs in designing specific interventions and monitoring them was very effective—enough so that we are going to continue the process.*
>
> Cathy Carson, Principal, St. Helens, Oregon

ACTION

Suggested Guidelines for Using Data

It is necessary to show that data are actually a reflection of what is taking place in classrooms. It's also important to guide people in interpreting and using data effectively. Here are some strategies:

1. Display data graphically in a variety of user-friendly formats—bar graphs, scatter plots, and tables—and use more than one type of display.

2. Provide data to teachers as early as possible during the school year.

3. Present and use data in a nonthreatening way. Keep it objective and let teachers do the analysis.

4. Provide training to help staff learn to interpret the data by doing the following:

    a. Look at strengths and celebrate them first, then ask the harder questions.
    b. Provide guiding questions or ideas of what to look for in the data.
    c. Offer guidance so teachers make the tie between data and the instructional program.

5. Ask site administrators, their supervisors, and appropriate professional development staff to attend data sessions along with teachers.

6. Add levels of complexity to data over time:
   a. Start with individual school data and then use district and state data to look at the larger picture.
   b. Disaggregate data to make comparisons by gender, ethnicity, and socioeconomic level.
   c. Encourage people—once they're comfortable with data—to make connections among district tests, state tests, and norm-referenced tests so that each measure isn't taken as an independent slice of data.

7. Work to build linkages among levels—rescaled data enable a teacher to look at an individual student's performance over time, from grade to grade.

8. When possible, provide teachers with their own printouts that they can highlight and refer to over and over rather than continuously going to the Web site (Sather, 2004).

PROVIDING ADDITIONAL RESOURCES ■

It is helpful to anticipate some of the additional resources that may be needed as teachers embark on the work of implementing PLTs. One school gave each PLT a small budget to buy supplies and provide student incentives such as guest speakers and field trips. Among other things, PLTs may require the following:

> *Data are to goals what signposts are to travelers; data are not end points, but data are essential to reaching them—the signposts on the road to school improvement.*
>
> Mike Schmoker, 1996

- Space—It is important to have a comfortable place to meet that is free of interruptions. This may be a teacher's classroom with a large worktable or a few desks pulled together. The teachers' lounge or workroom may be too public or busy for team meetings.
- Accessible storage—It may be helpful to designate a special file cabinet in the library to hold research articles and information about particular teaching strategies. When teams make their resources available to others, all teachers can benefit.
- Materials—Teams will need notebooks to store their meeting logs, training materials, student data, and research or information on specific strategies they are using to improve student learning. See tools H-4 and H-5 for a suggested format for team meeting agenda and log. Tool H-7 can be used by teams as they plan their work.
- Research—Easy access to research materials, both online and in the library, can make it easier for teachers to access and use valuable information. In some schools, the librarian can assist in locating research and teaching resources. In others, an administrator or department chair may provide some of the needed research.
- Professional books—Providing space and contents for a professional library indicates support for teachers as learners. The library may acquire subscriptions to a few of the most useful journals.

School leaders may also want to explore whether or not to use external support. It is often important to provide external support to both teachers and school leaders during the start-up phase of PLT training and implementation. An outside facilitator who is trained and fully understands the PLT process can help ensure the success of these efforts. The facilitator can bring new ideas and perspectives to the staff. When training is tailored to a specific school, the facilitator is often more successful at guiding activities that cover a difficult topic like building trust.

■ ESTABLISHING SUPPORTIVE ACCOUNTABILITY

Teachers need to be accountable for effectively using their time to implement the PLT process. This means that leaders set expectations for staff as well as for students. Working collaboratively with the staff prior to beginning PLT activities, leaders can define agreements that detail expectations and criteria for meeting them. They can also elicit staff buy-in to explicit expectations. Just as students are expected to arrive on time, attend classes regularly, and participate productively in lessons, teachers are also expected to have regular and punctual attendance and actively participate in their PLTs. Moreover, they need to use their PLT time effectively.

Keeping a meeting log helps document activities and provides an ongoing record of PLT activities and decisions. Teams are encouraged to document their thinking or reasons for specific decisions. In this way, meeting logs provide a sketch or map of the journey and can be used periodically to reflect on the process and accomplishments. School leaders can read and respond to logs in writing. This not only indicates their interest and keeps them informed about the work and progress of each PLT, it also provides an additional avenue for communication and support. Keeping a team notebook documents activities and maintains a rich record of the work. The notebook may contain meeting logs or minutes, team norms, focus questions, related research articles, information on chosen strategies and how they were used, assessment details, and other documents.

The entire school can benefit when leaders seek out and develop strategies that equip "teachers and leaders with the ability to transform educational accountability policies from destructive and demoralizing accounting drills into meaningful and constructive decision making in the classroom, school and district" (Reeves, 2004, p. 1). Real accountability occurs when teachers actively participate in the development, refinement, and reporting of accountability. In other words, teachers are collaboratively engaged in designing and implementing the accountability system. Reeves advocates for teachers taking the lead in documenting their practices in teaching and curriculum and the effects of those practices on student achievement. This means including systematic observation and reflection in each individual's teaching practice—tools that fit nicely with the work of PLTs.

Well-designed "classroom assessment created and scored by classroom teachers is the gold standard in educational accountability" (Reeves, 2004, p. 114). Engaging teachers in designing these assessments places their efforts on a par with the nationally prominent authors of tests. Viewing accountability in this way promotes teachers' connection to ongoing examination of their own teaching and their students' learning. This aligns with PLT goals as well as the administrative need to hold teachers accountable.

There are other strategies that establish accountability. One is scheduling three regular times during the school year for each PLT to share its work and progress with the entire staff. This can happen during a staff meeting or at another time specifically set aside for this type of sharing. Whole-school sharing contributes to developing and reinforcing a shared vision for school improvement focused on effective teaching and learning. It also keeps teams connected to each other and the larger system. Early on, teams may share their findings from examination of data and the direction they are choosing for further inquiry. At midyear, they may share progress, including some of the research they are using. Combined with the results of an analysis on schoolwide teaching practices, this information can stimulate thinking among teams. Near the end of the school year, teams are asked to make more formal presentations that include the focus question, related research, chosen strategies, common assessment, and results. For successful strategies, the team may make a case for other PLTs or even the entire school to adopt successful strategies.

Schoolwide Sharing	ACTION

- Schedule the first schoolwide sharing once teams have chosen a focus and are ready to implement classroom strategies. If each team reports on identified student needs, related research, the focus for their inquiry, and possible strategies that they plan to use, this may spark additional thinking in other teams. This can also contribute to greater cohesion in the school community.
- Schedule another schoolwide sharing midyear for teams to share progress and elicit support and possible suggestions for midcourse revisions if they encounter unexpected challenges.
- Near the end of the school year, schedule the final sharing and use this time to celebrate the work of all teams for the year. Remember, all strategies may not have been successful. In a trusting, safe climate, teams should be encouraged to share challenges and speculate on reasons for the failure of a specific strategy.
- If time permits, it can be very effective to have one monthly time when all teams meet as a group for less formal sharing.

KEY POINTS FOR CHAPTER 3 ■

Laying the Foundation Within the School Community

- Communicating with all constituents can help pave the way for success.
- All professional development activities need to be coherent and aligned with school and district goals.

- A leadership team can help develop staff buy-in to the change process.
- Sufficient time needs to be allocated and protected for PLT training and regular team meetings.
- It's essential to provide data along with training to interpret and apply that information.
- Supportive accountability helps sustain the work of PLTs.
- Schoolwide sharing connects teams to the larger system or community.

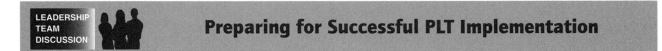

LEADERSHIP TEAM DISCUSSION

Preparing for Successful PLT Implementation

- Are we communicating necessary information to all constituents—teachers, support staff, union, school board, central administration, parents, community members? How are we doing this?
- Do we need to do more to build district support for our school as we move to institute PLTs?
- Does our school improvement plan include and support ongoing professional learning through the PLT process?
- Do we need to strengthen our leadership team?
- Is the leadership team serving as a collaborative role model?
- How are we modeling professional learning?
- Have we fully explored options for providing sufficient time for PLTs to meet? Specifically, how will we allocate and protect time for collaborative professional learning?
- What sources of data do we already have in place? Do we need additional access to data? Should we provide data in different formats? Do we need to provide additional training for staff to more effectively use data?
- Do we need to plan to provide additional teacher resources to support the PLTs?
- How will we establish accountability for teachers as they work in individual PLTs?
- What do we need to do to encourage and support teachers' self-reflection?
- When will we schedule schoolwide sharing? What guidelines do we need to establish to assure this time is productive?

Notes:

What About Leadership?

How do you develop and sustain a greater number of "system thinkers in action?" I call this breed of leader "the new theoretician." These are leaders at all levels of the system who proactively and naturally take into account and interact with larger parts of the system as they bring about deeper reform and help produce other leaders working on the same issues.

Michael Fullan, 2005, p. x

FOCUS OF THIS CHAPTER

- What is the role of school administrators in school change?
  - How do we develop instructional leadership?
  - What is our involvement with the teams?
- Why share leadership?
- What about teacher leadership?
- How do we sustain leadership when administrators leave?

School leaders play a crucial role in encouraging and fostering the development of professional learning communities in schools through professional learning teams (PLTs). School-site leadership should include teacher leaders as well as administrators. However, the research on leadership underscores the central importance of principals and other administrators in leading school change.

Leadership is widely regarded as a key factor in accounting for differences in the success with which schools foster the learning of their students. Indeed, the contribution of effective leadership is largest when it is needed most; there are virtually no documented instances of troubled schools being turned around in the absence of intervention by talented leaders. While other factors within the school also contribute to such turnarounds, leadership is the catalyst.

Kenneth Leithwood, Karen Seashore Louis, Stephen Anderson, & Kyla Wahlstrom, 2004, p. 17

■ ADMINISTRATORS AS LEADERS

Principals are central to productive school change. Their understanding and support are essential for the successful development of PLTs. In a study of professional learning communities—of which PLTs are a critical component—Hord (2004) notes that "transforming the school organization into a learning community can be done only with the leader's sanction and active nurturing of the entire staff's development as a community" (p. 8). Other researchers studying the connection between school leadership and student learning underscore the importance of principal leadership. "Successful school leaders influence student achievement through two important pathways—the support and development of effective teachers and the implementation of effective organizational processes" (Davis, Darling-Hammond, LaPointe, & Meyerson, 2005, p. 2). PLTs are one of the organizational processes that, when successfully put in place, help develop effective teachers.

In their meta-analysis of studies examining the effects of leadership on student achievement, Waters and colleagues demonstrate that there is indeed a "substantial relationship between leadership and student achievement" (Waters, Marzano, & McNulty, 2003, p. 3). They report that an increase in leadership abilities translates into a statistically significant increase in student achievement. Leaders need to "identify and focus on improving the school and classroom practices that are most likely to have a positive impact on student achievement in their school" (p. 5).

Leithwood and colleagues found that regardless of the approach to school reform, success depends on the motivations and capacities of local leadership. School leaders contribute to student learning indirectly, through their influence on other people. Success depends on leaders making judicious choices about where in the organization to spend their time and attention. The researchers (Leithwood, Louis, Anderson, & Wahlstrom, 2004) report the following:

- Leadership is second only to classroom instruction among all school-related factors that contribute to what students learn at school. The effects of leadership on student learning account for about a quarter of total school effects.
- Leadership effects are usually greatest where and when they are needed most. In other words, "demonstrated effects of successful leadership are considerably greater in schools that are in more difficult circumstances" (p. 5).

Morrissey and Cowan (2000) describe ways that principals create and sustain professional learning communities. Principals' actions to develop the following five dimensions "were crucial to the creation and sustenance of a professional learning community" (p. 45):

- *Developing collective values and vision* in the school by focusing on "doing what is best for students" and using the vision to develop and recruit quality staff

- *Supporting shared decision making* by establishing structures and processes that contribute to, promote, and increase decision making capacity of teachers over time
- *Promoting continuous learning* by communicating the value of learning, monitoring growth and progress, and connecting professional development to the school improvement goals
- *Encouraging collaboration* by providing time and support for collaboration and identifying potential outcomes of that collaboration
- *Providing support* by establishing clear expectations, creating opportunities to develop relationships among staff, devising structures for communication, and acknowledging the human capacity for change

In a study of five high-poverty districts making strides in improving student achievement, principals and teacher leaders were crucial to the districts' systems of instructional leadership. Principals were expected to act as the primary instructional leaders at the school sites. To this end, they were provided with training in observing classrooms, giving instructional feedback to teachers, and using data to analyze student performance and teaching strategies. They were also given guidance on building collaborative structures (Togneri & Anderson, 2003).

> *Administrators who use their authority to build a teacher community convey new expectations for teachers' work in the school, and they ensure that teachers have the time, space, and knowledge resources needed for collaborative work. They build trust and open communication among all teachers in the school.*
>
> Milbrey W. McLaughlin & Joan E. Talbert, 2006, p. 58

Instructional Leadership

Developing the instructional leadership capacity of school leaders has come to the forefront in school change in recent years. "Administrators, along with teachers, must be learners: questioning, investigating, and seeking solutions for school improvement and student achievement" (Hord, 2004, p. 8). In many districts, principals are expected to place a much higher priority on leading instruction and less on the management duties of their office. Some districts have shifted emphasis in their administrators' meetings from sharing information to training principals in some of the necessary instructional leadership skills such as conducting a walk-through and engaging teachers in learning-focused conversations (Sather, 2004). Instructional leadership does not mean that the principal is expected to become an expert in every content area. It does mean that she can recognize quality teaching and effective instruction that results in student engagement and learning. Leaders can also develop and support a culture of inquiry within the school. As they conduct an ongoing dialogue around school change efforts, they introduce teachers to new research and strategies from their own reading and training. They can frame their own focusing questions to guide a leadership PLT in following the established inquiry cycle. In this way, they model ongoing learning as well as lead the school thoughtfully through change that contributes to increased student learning.

Emphasizing the connection between instruction and leadership, Fullan (2001b) states the following:

The single most important factor ensuring that all students meet performance goals at the site level is the leadership of the principal—leadership being defined as *"the guidance and direction of instructional improvement."* Focusing on selecting principals who are instructionally focused is a necessary first step, followed by creating an intense, comprehensive system of professional development to promote their continued growth. (p. 126)

Fullan further recommends on-site coaching for principals to learn the strategies and behaviors they need to use with teachers in classrooms to improve student learning. Study groups, action research, and sharing experiences with other principals provide tangible support in ways that help develop instructional leadership skills. Many principals now position themselves as learners and take responsibility for their own professional development. In addition, capable school leaders place adult learning, along with student learning, at the center of all decisions in a school (National Association of Elementary School Principals, 2001).

Three sets of strategies make up the core of successful leadership and guide administrators as they support the successful implementation of PLTs:

1. Set directions and help colleagues develop shared understandings about the organization and its activities and goals.

2. Develop people; for example, offer intellectual stimulation, individualized support, and appropriate models of best practice and beliefs that are fundamental to the organization.

3. Redesign the organization in ways that support and sustain the performance of administrators and teachers, as well as students (Leithwood et al., 2004, pp. 8–9).

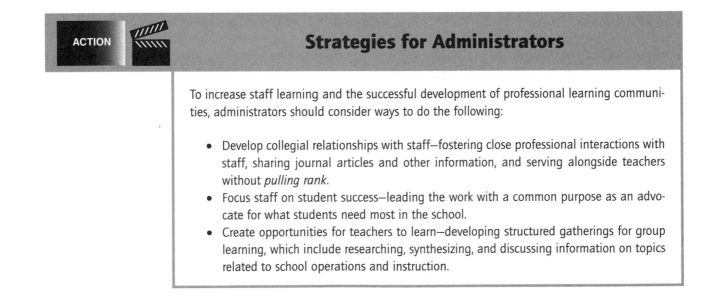

ACTION

Strategies for Administrators

To increase staff learning and the successful development of professional learning communities, administrators should consider ways to do the following:

- Develop collegial relationships with staff—fostering close professional interactions with staff, sharing journal articles and other information, and serving alongside teachers without *pulling rank*.
- Focus staff on student success—leading the work with a common purpose as an advocate for what students need most in the school.
- Create opportunities for teachers to learn—developing structured gatherings for group learning, which include researching, synthesizing, and discussing information on topics related to school operations and instruction.

- Invite teachers to help make and implement decisions—developing organizational structures to incorporate and support staff involvement in decisions for the school. This includes consulting with teachers, creating design teams or committees focused on specific issues, and choosing a theme for the year that guides teams' work with curriculum and instruction.
- Nurture new ways of operating—creatively altering school schedules to arrange time for staff planning and meeting; preparing teachers to use that time productively; and rearranging teacher assignments to increase teacher collegiality and support (Fleming, 2004, summarized from pp. 23–27).

Supporting PLTs

VOICES FROM THE FIELD

My role is to be a cheerleader for PLTs. I need to read the research so that I understand what is going on. I bought professional time for our PLT leaders so they could attend training during the school day. My job is also to keep the PLT process in front of the teachers, to remind them that this is the way we look at issues. PLT processes are now used in our other groups. Our group discussions sound more like those of a research team than they previously did. Our administrative team (counselors, the dean of students, the athletic director, vice principals, and principal) also function as a PLT. . . . I am now the new superintendent in this district, and I'm going to promote the use of the PLT model because it gives all teachers a voice and helps them understand that they are designing strategies that move us ahead.

Lonnie Barber, Former High School Principal,
Current Assistant Superintendent, Idaho

Being Visible Throughout the School

Administrators need to be out and about in the school, not cloistered in their office. It behooves administrators to establish relationships with the staff so they can walk into classrooms at various times without the pressures of evaluation. They can then experience teaching and learning as it happens. Teachers appreciate having administrators visit their classes and provide constructive feedback. It helps break down the sense of isolation that some teachers feel. Developing the walk-through process is one productive way to do this while strengthening instructional leadership knowledge and skills. Some secondary schools also build instructional leadership skills in their department chairs as part of professional development efforts.

The walk-through (Downey, Steffy, English, Frase, & Poston, 2004) is a structured process that specifically develops a snapshot of a group of classrooms at a particular moment in time. The walk-through can influence real change in schools by getting administrators close to the classroom and building their capacity to become instructional leaders. It is purposefully kept separate from teacher evaluation. The walk-through is usually conducted by the principal and an assistant principal or supervising administrator. It provides an opportunity to observe curriculum and teaching in action. After visiting each classroom, administrators can discuss their perceptions with each other to deepen their understanding of classroom teaching and learning. When the walk-through is well implemented and purposefully kept separate from evaluation, teachers appreciate involvement and input from their administrators (Sather, 2004).

Administrators do need to attend some of the individual PLT meetings, either as participant or observer, and provide relevant feedback and suggestions to teachers. They should resist the urge to take over and run the meeting in order to get teachers to focus on aspects of teaching that the principal may have identified. Remember, PLTs need to be led by teachers who then develop ownership and build their own leadership skills.

Provide Situational Leadership

Stay with the process during the early formative meetings. If necessary, assist a PLT that lacks clear leadership by facilitating and modeling leadership for a few meetings to ensure the team develops a culture. But as soon as possible, wean that team from your involvement and allow others to step forward as leaders. Identify potential leaders and support them in developing their leadership skills. This can only happen if they are provided with opportunities to practice their own leadership.

Darrel Burbank, Retired Elementary School Principal, Idaho

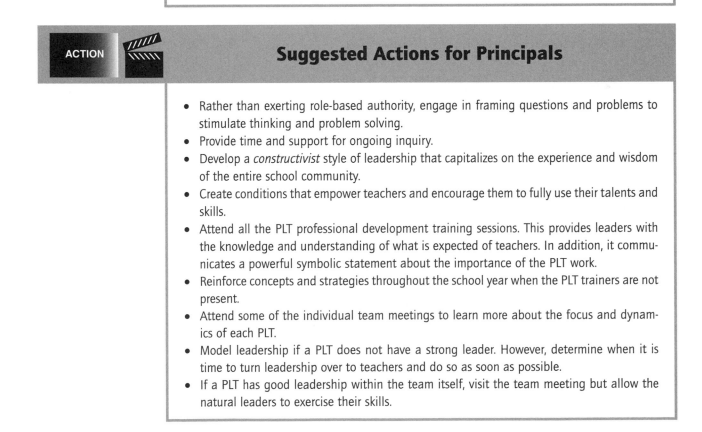

Suggested Actions for Principals

- Rather than exerting role-based authority, engage in framing questions and problems to stimulate thinking and problem solving.
- Provide time and support for ongoing inquiry.
- Develop a *constructivist* style of leadership that capitalizes on the experience and wisdom of the entire school community.
- Create conditions that empower teachers and encourage them to fully use their talents and skills.
- Attend all the PLT professional development training sessions. This provides leaders with the knowledge and understanding of what is expected of teachers. In addition, it communicates a powerful symbolic statement about the importance of the PLT work.
- Reinforce concepts and strategies throughout the school year when the PLT trainers are not present.
- Attend some of the individual team meetings to learn more about the focus and dynamics of each PLT.
- Model leadership if a PLT does not have a strong leader. However, determine when it is time to turn leadership over to teachers and do so as soon as possible.
- If a PLT has good leadership within the team itself, visit the team meeting but allow the natural leaders to exercise their skills.

SHARED AND FACILITATIVE LEADERSHIP ■

Principals have the power to affect student learning by setting a clear direction for change, focusing on success, and supporting staff learning. However, effective professional learning communities depend on an open and facilitative leadership style that demonstrates, in tangible terms, that every adult in the school—like every student—must engage in a learning process. Teachers as well as students benefit when they take ownership of their own learning. This evolves into taking ownership of the authority needed to create a better learning environment for students.

According to Hord (2004), in order to "foster shared leadership, the principal must encourage others to assume leadership roles and be able to recognize when staff, parents, or others are ready to take on leadership roles" (p. 8). Moller (2004) adds, "If professional learning communities provide the best hope for sustained school improvement, and shared leadership is a critical component of successful professional learning communities, then principals must be both willing to share leadership and able to develop conditions and communicate expectations that will advance shared leadership among school professionals" (p. 140). Thus, there is a need to refashion the old roles of principals and teachers into new ones to meet the current demands placed on schools and establish higher accountability for all. When teachers participate in an authentic professional community, they "develop norms of collegiality, openness, trust, experimentation, risk taking, and feedback. Teaching becomes more public and more open to critique and improvement; in turn, the teaching community promotes an expanded view of professional responsibility and accountability—a move from concerns about *my* students in *my* classroom to *our* students in *our* school" (Lieberman & Miller, 2004, p. 11).

Spillane, Halverson, and Diamond (2001) suggest, "school leadership is best understood as a distributed practice, 'stretched over' the school's social and situational contexts" (p. 23). This indicates that leadership is shared among people in different roles rather than neatly parceled out. It becomes a dynamic interaction between multiple leaders (and followers) and the potentially shifting context. This means that the capacity for leadership exists within and among all members of the larger school community: administrators, teachers, parents, and students. "Many, rather than few, have a share of responsibility for the shared purpose, a view of leadership requiring the redistribution of power and authority toward those who hold expertise, and not necessarily privileging those with formal titles" (Copland, 2003, p. 378). In fact, McLaughlin and Talbert (2001) found that successful principals worked in collaboration with teacher leaders and with respect for the teaching culture. The leadership of these principals came "from a strong commitment to making the school work for their students and building teachers' commitment and capacity to pursue this vision collectively" (p. 118).

This emerging concept of "distributed leadership" encourages schools to have multiple leaders, each exercising control over the areas in which they possess the greatest expertise. Collectively, principals, teachers, staff, and other stakeholders set direction, assess progress, and improve teaching.

Cleveland Initiative for Education, 2004, p. 13

■ TEACHER LEADERSHIP

Central to an expanded vision of teachers as "researchers, meaning makers, scholars, and inventors" (Lieberman & Miller, 2000) is the concept of teachers as leaders who can make a difference in schools (p. 11). The growth of teacher leaders was an unexpected and valuable outcome of this PLT process as we field tested in schools. Teacher leadership is fostered and supported initially by involving teachers on the leadership team that plans and develops PLTs in the school. Teacher leadership is expanded as individuals work in teams to move through the inquiry cycle (see Chapter 1). Since PLTs are teacher led, leadership emerges and is nurtured both by the individual PLTs and by administrators who work closely with the leadership team to oversee school reform efforts. There is a strong role for both administrators and teacher leaders as the organization shifts to become a professional learning community. "Administrators are viewed as leaders of leaders. Teachers are viewed as transformational leaders . . . . [Teachers] transform students' lives, motivate and inspire students, and get students to do things they never thought they could do" (Eaker, DuFour, & DuFour, 2002, pp. 22–23).

> *This PLT accomplished more research and decision making than any other team I've been on. It's been a slow growing process that finally led to results.*
>
> Elementary School Teacher, Reading PLT, Idaho

The PLT structure and processes align well with two communities of practice—the National Writing Project and Leadership for Tomorrow's Schools—that demonstrate the research on teacher leadership as it plays out in real life (Lieberman & Miller, 2004). "Both organizations enact the tenets of professional learning within a community of practice: learning is experiential and collective; it is context-driven and context-sensitive; and it occurs through social participation . . . . [Both organizations] rely on a set of social practices that promote learning, meaning, and identity and that assist teachers in coming to view themselves as teacher leaders and in learning to act the part" (pp. 33–34).

Implementing the PLT process helps build the capacity of teacher leaders. However, it is not sufficient to train teachers and leave them to their own devices to develop leadership. It requires a conscious effort on the part of administrators to encourage, support, and sometimes make additional leadership training available to their teachers. In addition, widely distributing leadership among teachers can help ensure continuation of reform strategies—such as the PLT process—even when there is a new principal.

While supporting the process in multiple ways, it is important that administrators ensure that PLTs are teacher led. There may be times when the principal disagrees with the PLT's line of inquiry. She may make suggestions or ask thoughtful questions to stimulate a learning discussion. However, it is essential to let the teachers lead by owning the process. They need to be encouraged to think outside the box at times and to try new strategies. Principals reinforce the concept of teachers as professionals when they set and communicate their expectations for teamwork and then support teachers as they proceed to focus on student learning and classroom instruction in their PLTs. Principals put the *P* in PLT when they support their staff in developing their own leadership skills and encourage teams to be teacher led.

We recommend that each PLT assign teachers different roles for each meeting. Suggested roles are facilitator, recorder, timekeeper, and process watcher. Having role badges serves as a tangible reminder to use and rotate these roles. While there will often be a natural leader on a team, rotation allows each teacher to experience leading the group and to hone his or her own skills in that area. Rotating roles also shifts responsibility for taking notes to maintain the record of meeting activities. Changing the process watcher encourages everyone to pay attention and follow the team's working agreements or norms. Rotating roles also allows team members to experience the work of the team from multiple perspectives. (See Tool H-6, Defining Team Roles.)

Tool H-6 Defining Team Roles

TOOL

At one time or another, all members of your Professional Learning Team (PLT) will fulfill the roles your PLT establishes. Having PLT members take responsibility for various critical team functions helps ensure that they are recognized and accomplished. In this way, individual members learn how to complete necessary tasks, and your PLT avoids becoming dominated by an individual with a stronger leadership background or tendencies. The PLT is also more likely to be effective when members assume these roles on a rotating basis each time the PLT convenes. Rotating roles ensures that all members have the opportunity to develop their leadership skills and exposes the PLT to different leadership styles.

Roles should remain flexible within the PLT. New roles may be created, and old ones retired as the needs of the team change. Initially, PLT roles might include the following:

Facilitator: Helps the team set the agenda, time, and place of the meeting and sends agenda out in advance and keeps discussions on topic

The Facilitator makes statements such as, "Let's stay on task" and asks, "Any more ideas?"

Recorder: Keeps track of the team's comments and decisions and through the written record, creates a group memory and facilitates sharing of information outside the team

The Recorder makes statements such as, "Let me make sure I wrote this down correctly," and asks, "What are our main points?"

Timekeeper: Makes sure each agenda item has an assigned length of time and keeps team apprised of how well it is moving through the agenda and suggests and manages any impromptu adjustments to the agenda

The Timekeeper makes statements such as, "We have five more minutes" and asks, "Should we discuss this topic now or wait until our next meeting?"

Process Observer: Reminds team of the ground rules and norms and notes when acceptable group procedures are and are not being followed

The Process Observer makes statements such as, "Today we stayed on task" and "We didn't allow equal air time."

You may choose to add additional roles.

In some schools, an outside facilitator is used to train the entire staff in the PLT process. However, other schools have chosen to train a cadre of their own teachers as facilitators to train their colleagues. This helps transform these teachers and facilitators into instructional leaders.

A word of caution: While it is important for administrators to allow PLTs to be teacher led and to develop teacher leaders, this does not mean abandoning teachers or teams. It behooves school administrators to remain involved with the PLTs and to be aware of the direction each team takes: their focus questions, suggested strategies, implementation efforts, methods of assessment, and successes. This interest in and knowledge of each PLT opens the door for administrators to provide ongoing support to teachers in their efforts to enhance their own instruction and provide deeper, more productive learning opportunities for students.

VOICES FROM THE FIELD

Developing Teacher Leaders

It is incredibly important to develop the capacity of all staff members, to develop teachers as leaders, and to help them develop their process and the school plan so clearly that it won't matter who the principal is. Thus, we need a variety of teacher leaders: PLT representatives, summer school leaders, teachers serving on the site council, and department coordinators looking at district curriculum with some of them sitting on curriculum adoption committees.

Christine Lynch, Middle School Principal, Washington

ACTION

Encouraging Teacher Leadership

To effectively use teacher leadership, school and district leaders can provide support by doing the following:

1. Guide the staff in articulating student learning and school improvement goals and related priorities for development and action.

2. Generate possible ways that teachers can lead efforts related to accomplishing these goals.

3. Match the "unique and varied leadership capacities" of individual teachers with the "unique and varied leadership functions" (National Staff Development Council, 2001).

4. Encourage all teachers to develop and use their inherent leadership abilities; after all, each teacher is a leader in her own classroom. One way to do this is to enhance teachers' skills through leadership training.

SUSTAINING LEADERSHIP ■

What happens when the strong, supportive principal leaves the school for another position or retirement? Hargreaves and Fink (2006) have written extensively about intentionally sustaining successful leadership in order to maintain improvement in a school and district. They describe seven principles of sustainability in educational change and leadership: depth, length, breadth, justice, diversity, resourcefulness, and conservation. While all seven principles are important, length and breadth are of particular significance to providing ongoing support for collaborative structures in schools. Sustainable leadership lasts—the most valuable aspects of change are advanced from one leader to the next. The concept of breadth is closely aligned with length in that it depends on the leadership of many and is distributed throughout the school and district (pp. 18–19). Thus, change is not contingent upon a single powerful and charismatic leader who may leave a void when departing the school. With planning and forethought, leadership develops among many individuals, represents shared values and vision for change, and becomes sustainable.

Building on the work of Peter Senge (1990) and others, Fullan (2005) advocates sustaining leadership by developing and maintaining an ever-widening circle of systems thinkers. These brief references to systems theory in no way do justice to this complex theory. Suffice it to say that educators, hoping to improve learning for all students by stimulating lasting change in schools, can benefit by serious consideration and application of these principles.

As we move to thinking about sustaining PLTs as well as leadership, let's visit one school implementing PLTs. As with all schools, their process involved challenges along the way. This particular school chose to use the trainer of trainers model with ongoing support from NWREL.

VIGNETTE: A PROFESSIONAL LEARNING TEAM IN ACTION

For once the fifth-grade team was working collaboratively. We all grew in respect for each other. I know I'm a better teacher because of it.

Maria Heath, fifth-grade teacher, St. Helens, Oregon

During the 2006–2007 school year, Heath and two other teacher leaders at Lewis and Clark Intermediate School guided their colleagues through the PLT inquiry process. In addition to developing stronger relationships in the workplace, all four teams at this school witnessed a healthy growth in student learning, demonstrated in pre- and post-tests in reading or math.

St. Helens, population 11,640, is a rapidly growing community attracting commuters from Portland, Oregon, 30 miles to the southeast. Lewis and Clark Intermediate served all third- through fifth-grade students in the community. Almost 40 percent of the student population received free or reduced-price lunch. Although the school made adequate yearly progress in 2005–2006, teachers felt more needed to be done to boost their lowest performing students.

Heath and Barbara Shriver, a fourth-grade teacher, discovered PLTs while searching online for professional development opportunities. At their own personal expense, they attended the first installment of a two-part institute held by the Northwest Regional Educational Laboratory (NWREL) during the summer of 2006. This first training introduced participants to the PLT Inquiry cycle (see Chapter 1), collaboration tools, strategies for examining their own achievement data, developing a focus for their inquiry, locating and evaluating research, and selecting and implementing proven practices. They also developed specific plans for working with the rest of the staff back at the school. This training prepared them to guide colleagues halfway through the inquiry cycle. Heath and Shriver were so inspired by what they learned that they lobbied Assistant Principal Cathy Carson to consider implementing PLTs at Lewis and Clark. Carson was receptive to the idea and asked third-grade teacher Kathleen Alexander to join them at the next training. Since administrative support is crucial to the success of any school change effort, Carson's involvement was a critical piece of the equation at Lewis and Clark. The fall institute provided an opportunity to come together again and share successes and challenges as well as analyze current and potential teaching practices, learn more about implementing changes, developing and analyzing classroom assessments, and preparing for schoolwide sharing and celebration.

At the institute, Carson and the three teachers received a thorough grounding and tools to complete the rest of the PLT inquiry cycle. Back at the school, these teacher leaders guided their teams through the collaborative inquiry cycle. However, they discovered they needed support along the way, which was provided by NWREL trainer Jacqueline Raphael. According to Heath, these phone and e-mail conversations were important to the facilitators. Attesting to the value of having external support, Heath reported, "We checked in throughout the year. There were times when I was overwhelmed with the whole thing. It was nice to know I could ask for advice."

Mandatory or Optional Teams? One question that the school struggled with early on was whether PLT membership should be mandatory or optional. This is a dilemma that every leadership or administrative team must address prior to starting the PLT process. For the first year, they decided to grow their teams over time—encouraging rather than requiring participation. As a result, about a quarter of the school's teachers declined to participate. The school's four PLTs served as a pilot program for the district as well as the school. The teams included one at the fifth-grade level, two for fourth-grade teachers, and one for third-grade teachers. Two of the PLTs included special education teachers, and one counted the librarian among its members.

Finding Time. Time is always an issue for schools, and Lewis and Clark was no exception as it dealt with scheduling team meetings and time for leaders to get together to support each other and plan trainings. All Lewis and Clark teachers—whether or not they belonged to PLTs—met in their own grade levels monthly during three hours of required professional development time. The four PLTs additionally met at least twice a month after school but still within the regular contract day. They sometimes met informally in addition to their regularly scheduled meetings.

During part of the three-hour grade-level meetings, PLTs reported on their progress and shared strategies and lessons with their colleagues. Thus, even those teachers who declined to participate were exposed to the PLT activities, although they were not required to implement the chosen strategies. In the 2007–2008 school year, Lewis and Clark required all teachers to implement the strategies and lessons designed in PLTs, while PLT membership remained optional.

Heath, Shriver, and Alexander also met monthly with Cathy Carson to plan for these monthly three-hour professional development sessions. These meetings included time to troubleshoot PLT challenges while Carson provided support for these teachers. The three lead teachers also received release time to work with colleagues, modeling or observing teaching strategies and providing feedback and classroom support. These team leaders set the agenda, made sure that everyone on the team had a role, and rotated those roles. The minutes of each meeting were sent monthly to the principal.

Using Data. Providing data can be a challenge for administrators as schools embark on implementing collaborative inquiry to enhance student learning. With the national emphasis on high-stakes testing, it might be assumed that schools are data rich. However, annual test results are insufficient to guide essential teaching decisions and influence classroom practice. Data need to be presented with enough guidance so that all teachers can make use of the information. Teachers must be able to drill down into data to access relevant information on their own students. While the progress made by the entire school and district is important, identifying the learning challenges of one's own students is critical for teachers' instructional decisions.

Teachers at Lewis and Clark use Mastery in Motion,* which provides instant results and assists teachers in getting the kind of information they need. Mastery in Motion is an online database that makes state and district assessments and classroom work sample data accessible. Information may be used to evaluate programs, plan instruction, and inform students and parents about progress.

With this electronic tool, Lewis and Clark's PLTs were able to easily manipulate the data to identify the lowest 30 percent of their students and zoom in on specific skills that these students were missing. All PLTs chose to focus their inquiry and select strategies for reaching this group in the belief that helping these children would improve learning for all students. According to Carson, "Having a uniform data gathering tool enabled the teachers to make sure they were focusing on the target group and comparing similar groups, in fact comparing apples to apples."

For Lewis and Clark—as well as all schools' PLTs—ongoing, formative, classroom-level assessment becomes an important part of the inquiry cycle. It provides timely information about student progress that informs instructional decisions. PLTs use this information to regularly gauge the effects of their selected teaching strategies.

It takes time to develop meaningful assessments. Waiting for standardized test results does not adequately inform daily classroom practice based on shifting student needs. At Lewis and Clark, some of the teams were relying on annual TESA (Technology Enhanced Student Assessment) results as their bottom line measure. Since this test is computerized, results are available immediately. However, the teachers were thrown a curve ball when the state of Oregon eliminated the TESA midyear, wiping out the potential for pre- and post-test comparisons using the same measure. The teachers were then forced to develop, as a team, their own post-test measures related to the specific skills they were focusing on. Fifth-grade teachers confronted this dilemma and developed their own test using items from their new reading curriculum. They administered this test to all fifth-grade students, those receiving the treatment as well as the others. In this way, they compared the results of PLT efforts with students from those teachers not engaged in the PLT process.

---

*Mastery in Motion. (1998–2007). www.2mim.com

Other Challenges. Teams found it difficult to locate research related to their chosen topics. For the most part, they chose to rely on popular education journals for information rather than going to some of the peer-juried publications. With time, teams can begin to seek out more rigorous research to inform their work.

In their final presentations, teams recommended slowing down the process to go more deeply into each phase of the PLT inquiry cycle. However, this realization was only made possible by the first-hand experience of meeting and collaborating in teams. With many extended efforts at making change in classrooms to enhance student learning, there is an aha moment near the end of the year when the scope of work and details needed for success shift into focus. Moving toward this deeper understanding is supported by regular, ongoing team reflection and preparation for whole school presentations.

Celebrating Results. At the end of the year, the teams held a celebration to share their results with the entire school staff as well as the district superintendent and the curriculum director. Each team gave a PowerPoint presentation detailing their research—the focusing question that guided their inquiry, selected strategies, and pre- and post-test results. All the teams reported positive gains by the target group—the students scoring in the lowest 30 percent—as well as the entire class. As one team member said, "It was work, but it was work that made me feel good. I am very willing to do that work because it is productive. We saw an increase in student performance!"

The fifth-grade team identified making inferences as their most pressing student learning challenge. Thus, they came up with a focusing question: Will graphic organizers help develop our students' ability to infer information from text? Members used the research on graphic organizers from McMackin and Witherell (2005). Heath reported, "A lot of us really weren't sure that having focused instruction in one strand would really make that big a difference. We were all surprised at our test results." (See Table 3 for results. These are taken from the PowerPoint presentations made by each team.)

Table 3   Fifth-Grade PLT Results

70% is a passing score	
Receiving PLT Intervention	**No PLT Intervention**
78% passed the post-assessment	69% passed the post-assessment
Average score: 77.5%	Average score: 72.1%
Average score for lowest 30%* of students was 64.8%	Average score for lowest 30% of students was 57.9%

*The 30% of students scoring lowest in early data examination were the target group. For this assessment, their teachers compared the progress of those lowest 30% students who had teachers in PLTs to the lowest 30% students who did not have teachers in PLTs.

The fourth grade formed two PLTs: the math team worked with statistics and probability, while the reading team targeted students' ability to locate information in informational text. (See Tables 4 and 5 for results.)

Table 4 Fourth-Grade Mathematics PLT Results

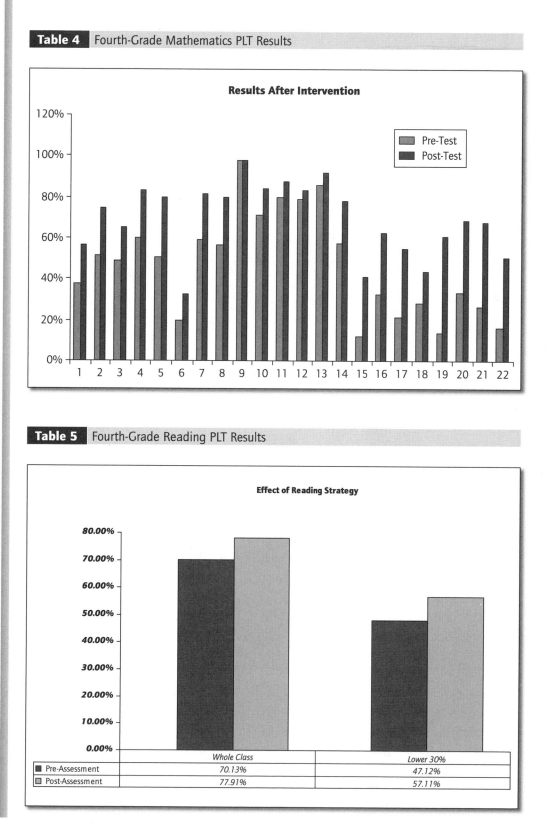

Table 5 Fourth-Grade Reading PLT Results

	Whole Class	Lower 30%
Pre-Assessment	70.13%	47.12%
Post-Assessment	77.91%	57.11%

The third grade homed in on "creating authentic learning experiences for students to understand the purpose of different types of informational text and read them to perform a task." (See Tables 6 and 7 for results.)

Table 6 Third-Grade Results

	Number of students	Average score pre-test	Average score post-test	Percent gain	Number of students with score below 70% pre-test	Number of students with score below 70% post-test
Whole class	124	81	89	8	25	17
Lowest 30%	28	67	78	11	12	7

Table 7 Third-Grade Assessment Data

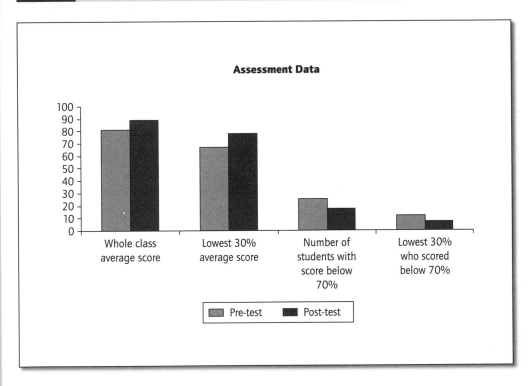

In addition to increased student learning during the pilot year, Heath notes, "the trust level among teachers improved, especially those on PLTs." She believes there is now a greater focus on using research because that is a part of the whole equation. And, she says, "Teachers now talk about their teaching or their lessons, not about student deficiencies."

Cathy Carson became principal of Lewis and Clark at the end of the 2006–2007 school year when her predecessor retired. As a powerful ally of PLTs, Carson is committed to continuing the process. "Our professional learning community is now teacher led," she says. "We have a group of teachers who understand the PLT process, are invested in it, and are willing to put in their own professional time. They have more frequent interaction with data and do more classroom assessment. The collaboration piece put everything together, and PLTs helped us focus on the whole-student achievement piece. That was clearly the missing link in using the data and creating and applying appropriate strategies."

Perhaps in the best validation of the process, several of the teachers who didn't participate in PLTs e-mailed Carson after the end-of-year celebration. They signed on to participate fully in the process during the coming year.

KEY POINTS FOR CHAPTER 4 ■

What About Leadership?

- Administrators have a central role in creating conditions that lead to student learning and achievement in their schools.
- Developing instructional leadership supports PLT implementation and contributes to teacher and student learning along with change efforts.
- Shared and facilitative leadership help develop teacher leaders and contribute to the success of PLTs; this expands the principal's role as a leader of leaders.
- Teacher leadership needs to be cultivated and nurtured as PLTs are implemented.
- Leadership needs to expand in ways that ensure sustainability with administrator turnover.

Developing Leadership That Supports Schoolwide Learning

LEADERSHIP TEAM DISCUSSION

- Have we articulated a collective vision? Do all staff members understand and believe in that vision?
- As leaders, what are we doing that contributes to student learning and achievement?
- How are we building our own instructional leadership capacity?
- What do we need to put in place to develop or expand shared leadership?
- What structures already exist to facilitate shared decision making? What else do we need to do to support that process?
- What can we do to develop and support teacher leaders?
- How are we promoting the concept of continuous learning for adults as well as for students?
- Are we intentionally creating sustainable leadership?
- Are there other ways we can provide support for collaboration?
  1. Have we articulated clear expectations?
  2. Are we developing relationships among staff members?
  3. What structures for communication are in place? Do we need additional avenues for communication?
- How can we expand our capacity as *systems thinkers in action*?

Notes:

5

Supporting the Work of PLTs

Professional learning communities are paradoxical. They need to focus on the process of learning as well as on measurable results, on long-term transformation as well as on immediate achievement gains, and on being persistent about improvement as well as patient in waiting for the outcome.

Andy Hargreaves, 2007, cited
in Foreword to Hord and Sommers, p. xi

FOCUS OF THIS CHAPTER

- What supports the success of PLTs?
- What can we do to reinforce PLT strategies and skills?
- How do we ensure that PLTs are led by teachers?
- How can we use a rubric to support PLT implementation?
- What do we need to know about potential challenges?
- Why celebrate?

■ SUCCESSFUL PLTs

A review of current literature on effective professional development models, professional learning communities, and teacher learning reveals eight factors that support the successful implementation of PLTs. These factors should be viewed as interdependent and equally important. See Tool H-11 for a master of these factors. This can be used to stimulate discussion among the leadership team, with teachers and even with central office administrators. Discussions may center on the meaning of each factor as well as how to assure the concept is part of the action plan for PLT implementation.

Tool H-11 Factors Supporting the Success of PLTs

TOOL

1. There is *collective participation and collaboration* that involves groups of teachers working together to solve problems and refine practice to improve learning for all students.

2. Professional learning is *content rich and student focused;* that is, teacher learning provides opportunities for teachers to develop strong expertise in the content areas they teach and in understanding how students learn that subject area.

3. Professional learning is *teacher led.* It is learning that addresses real problems teachers face in their classrooms and involves individual as well as collective reflection and inquiry into professional practice.

4. There is ample *time and duration* for professional learning. Professional learning must be sustained over time and involve a substantial number of contact hours.

5. Professional learning occurs in a *data-rich* environment where teachers use multiple sources of information to analyze student learning goals against student performance.

6. There is *strong, supportive, and shared leadership* for professional learning. The role of the principal is vital. Sharing leadership with teachers, developing collaborative decision-making processes, and cultivating opportunities and structures for teacher learning are examples of practices that support PLTs.

7. *External support* such as district-level or external facilitators is important for teachers to be exposed to fresh ideas, approaches, and perspectives that challenge traditional thinking.

8. PLTs are one component of a *coherent plan* for improving student success. Coherence means that professional learning is part of a larger school improvement effort and that it is planned over multiple years, focused on specific goals tied to student learning.

Information relating to these factors can be found throughout this guide. In addition, school leaders can consider the following actions to further support the work of PLTs:

- Model tools, strategies, and professional learning.
- Ensure that individual PLTs are led by teachers.
- Anticipate and prepare for challenges.
- Emphasize the importance of self-reflection.
- Celebrate, celebrate, celebrate.

> *Many teachers need to experience cooperative professional inquiry before they will commit to it.*
>
> Bruce Joyce, 2004, p. 80

REINFORCING PLT STRATEGIES AND SKILLS ■

School leaders make a powerful statement about the value of collaboration when they attend and participate in all training sessions and use the PLT strategies learned in workshops in their other meetings. Following an agenda, keeping a log (or minutes) of meetings, posting minutes in a public place, and using defined team roles all reinforce collaboration skills. In addition to developing working agreements or norms in each PLT, the school can benefit from a jointly developed set of schoolwide agreements that are posted and reinforced. Reflecting on how well they follow these working agreements helps everyone become a productive team member. Encourage the entire staff to share responsibility for monitoring norms and speaking up when they feel the agreements are not being followed. Simply put, all of these strategies lead to more effective and collaborative meetings, and teachers can also use them in their classrooms with students.

Leaders can model and reinforce the value of ongoing learning and research use by engaging in their own reading, sharing key concepts from reading with staff, and providing current research to support the specific focus of each PLT. Principals in the schools studied by Hord (2004) were continuous learners. "Their ongoing personal and professional development activities informed their responses to change and allowed them to transfer their continuous learning practices to their staffs in order to create a community of professional learners" (pp. 20–21). They were continually engaged in reading, workshops, networking, and sharing new ideas with their staff members. They repeatedly scanned the horizon for new information to improve learning and achieve student success and applied information at their schools, intentionally modeling learning and its application. Following this model, leaders can build capacity among staff. They can copy and distribute pertinent articles as well as provide time at staff meetings to discuss current research. Leaders can attend conferences and share what they learn with staff. They should encourage teachers to pursue other professional development opportunities and provide ways for those teachers to share their experiences with the rest of the staff.

ACTION

Steps for Leaders

- Incorporate PLT strategies into other school activities. Using these strategies in staff and other committee meetings reinforces them.
- Use team roles and role badges in meetings to infuse them into the school culture. The principal can keep a set of role badges in the office for easy access.
- Develop and use schoolwide working agreements (norms) and a common process for decision making during staff and committee meetings.
- Provide additional resources such as a quiet place for PLTs to meet, notebooks to store meeting logs and other team documents, and books and journals for a professional library.
- Provide access to research on best practices and classroom strategies. Enlist the assistance of the librarian or an administrator to search out appropriate research early on while teachers are becoming accustomed to the process.
- Provide space to store materials that may be used by more than one PLT; look for common space and provide a file cabinet and bookshelves in the library or teachers' workroom.

- Acknowledge conflict and use it as an opportunity for growth.
- Provide clear expectations about the following:
  - Team accountability
  - Meeting times and the outcomes of meetings
  - Working with a specific question to guide the team's inquiry and maintaining a focus on student learning
  - Ensuring coherence with schoolwide and district goals

Provide Resources

VOICES FROM THE FIELD

Our role is to support the staff by providing resources as well as to hold them accountable—making them form that focus question and give it back to us, then work with them to stay focused. We also help classroom teachers who don't have a lot of time to read research. I often provided resources by suggesting research that teachers could access. I located Web sites and gave them books.

Carol McCloy, Former Assistant High School
Principal, Current Elementary Principal, Idaho

ENSURING THAT PLTs ARE TEACHER LED ■

Administrators hold an important central role in ensuring both the success of PLTs and the resulting increase in the academic achievement of students. They are guardians of the vision for school change that leads to success. How, then, do they cede leadership for PLTs to teachers? They need to be involved with the teams in order to understand both the academic focus and the interpersonal dynamics of their staff. Knowing when to overtly lead and when to back off requires thoughtful observation and a considered exercise in judgment. There are no hard and fast rules for this task. However, ensuring sufficient teacher representation on the leadership team and then working closely with that team can make a difference. Attending all training workshops and some of the individual team meetings provides the administrator with information about the focus for each team and their ability to work collaboratively. With a large staff, administrators can share responsibility for connecting with individual teams. Listening carefully to staff and observing teachers in their classrooms, as well as in meetings, helps administrators identify, develop, and support leadership skills in their staff.

> *It is now clear that most schools and teachers cannot produce the kind of learning demanded by the new reforms—not because they do not want to, but because they do not know how, and the systems they work in do not support their efforts to do so.*
>
> Linda Darling-Hammond, 1996, p. 7

Prior to actually forming PLTs, think about—and decide ahead of time—how teachers will select into teams. We recommend balancing the needs of individuals with school goals by providing choice with guidance and using clear criteria. We believe that allowing teachers choice will likely result in a higher level of participation and implementation. After carefully examining data, teachers develop focus questions that provide direction for their inquiry and guide their next steps. Grouping into PLTs based on these areas of interest has obvious advantages. It contributes to teachers' sense of empowerment and commitment to the work of their specific PLT.

However, some schools have consciously developed interdisciplinary PLTs based on pre-existing teacher groupings. Other schools—especially secondary schools—form PLTs by content area. Still other PLTs form according to grade level. It behooves administrators to involve the leadership team and, when possible, the entire teaching staff in making this decision.

It is important to understand that for many teachers learning to work collaboratively while they examine and share their own classroom practice can be challenging and even threatening. Some teachers are natural collaborators and take to this work immediately. Others may withhold judgment or even resist the process. Just as each school has its own specific context, each PLT will have its own personality and working style. Every PLT may progress at a different pace with varying degrees of enthusiasm. It takes time to develop an understanding of and confidence in the PLT process.

One caveat here: For PLTs to be effective, teachers need to own the process. While the administrator must ensure coherence with school and district goals, teachers need to know they have some control over the conditions of their own work. As Rosenholtz (1989) underscores, norms of collaboration develop when "principals structure them in the workplace by offering ongoing invitations for substantive decision making and faculty interaction" (p. 44).

In their zeal to move the school forward, some administrators lay down edicts that can undermine teachers' sense of efficacy. The following advice from two administrators who have experienced the PLT process in their own schools contains valuable suggestions.

VOICES FROM THE FIELD	**Letting Teachers Control the Team**

You have to believe that if you give more responsibility to teachers and those in the frontlines, it will work. If you are serious about developing PLTs, you need to create conditions that empower teachers. Become a better listener and let teachers do the talking. You may have significant experience, but let the teachers talk first. Allow them to feel comfortable sharing their ideas. At times you can guide the conversation and act as a facilitator to make sure everyone talks but do not dominate the meeting. Back off and let the dynamics of the PLT develop.

On the other hand without strong administrative leadership, PLTs can lag. They need encouragement. They need to feel that what they are doing is important. Administrators can help people move forward by asking them to report or present at staff meetings on a regular basis. When the PLT begins to focus on solutions, the administrator can come in and support what they are doing. Give them research information and data but allow them to establish their own focus and direction. The solution then belongs to them. Try to get those teachers who want to be told what to do to start coming out on their own.

Darrel Burbank, Former Elementary School Principal, Idaho

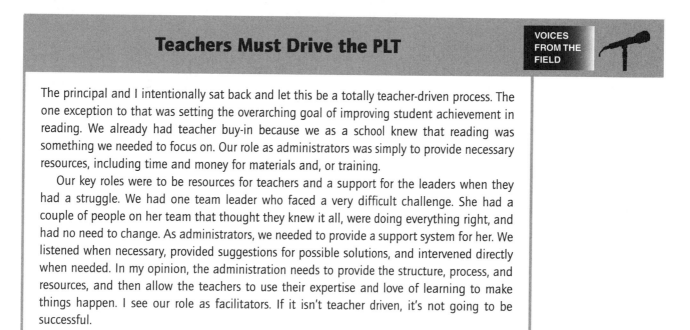

Teachers Must Drive the PLT

VOICES FROM THE FIELD

The principal and I intentionally sat back and let this be a totally teacher-driven process. The one exception to that was setting the overarching goal of improving student achievement in reading. We already had teacher buy-in because we as a school knew that reading was something we needed to focus on. Our role as administrators was simply to provide necessary resources, including time and money for materials and, or training.

Our key roles were to be resources for teachers and a support for the leaders when they had a struggle. We had one team leader who faced a very difficult challenge. She had a couple of people on her team that thought they knew it all, were doing everything right, and had no need to change. As administrators, we needed to provide a support system for her. We listened when necessary, provided suggestions for possible solutions, and intervened directly when needed. In my opinion, the administration needs to provide the structure, process, and resources, and then allow the teachers to use their expertise and love of learning to make things happen. I see our role as facilitators. If it isn't teacher driven, it's not going to be successful.

Rebecca Smith, Assistant Middle School Principal, Oregon

USING A RUBRIC TO ENCOURAGE REFLECTION ■

As we developed tools to support PLT implementation, we designed a rubric to provide transparency around the process and to help PLTs understand how to implement key PLT activities. This can be used early on in the journey to help PLTs understand where they are heading. It also assists teams to reflect over time as well as to identify and address challenges. The six dimensions of the rubric are based on the key activities undertaken by successful PLTs.

- PLT is supported by school organization and leadership.
- PLT uses data.
- PLT shares and reflects on classroom practice.
- PLT studies and uses research.
- PLT changes classroom practice.
- PLT uses collaborative and teamwork skills.

Teams may use the rubric to reflect on their process and self-evaluate their own progress. Skillful use of the rubric supports effective PLT functioning. We discourage its use in any formal evaluation of teachers or teams. This can mitigate its usefulness for self-evaluation.

This tool has several uses. First off, individual teams may take one dimension at a time and individually rate where they perceive the team is functioning. They then share ratings and open it up to discussion by the whole team. Reaching consensus on ratings is not important. The value lies in discussing individual perceptions and reasons for the rating. Discussing differing impressions of strengths and weaknesses can lay the groundwork for selecting actions leading to improvement, both for the team and their students. However, it is important to use *safe strategies* to guide this discussion. Teams can brainstorm ahead of time what they need to contribute to an honest discussion about team strengths and weaknesses. They may develop a set of norms to guide these discussions, or change or add to their team's *working agreements*. Remember, this discussion is much more valuable than reaching agreement on the numerical ratings.

The rubric follows and can also be found as Tool H-12 in a reproducible format.

**Professional Learning Team
Implementation Rubric**

**Developed by Jacqueline Raphael, Northwest
Regional Educational Laboratory**

PLT Name: _____

School: _____

Directions: For each page, please place an X on the most accurate rating (level 1, 2, 3, 4, or 5) corresponding to each feature listed in the horizontal rows.

Place the X over the text if marking levels 1, 3, or 5 and in the blank box if marking levels 2 or 4.

Thank you.

(1) Our PLT is well supported by the school organization and leadership.

Components	Level 1	Level 2	Level 3	Level 4	Level 5
Dedicating sufficient time for PLTs	Our school dedicates little or no time to PLTs.		Our school dedicates some time (e.g., 60 minutes every other week) to PLTs, but that time is not part of the regular daily schedule and is sometimes used for other purposes.		Our school dedicates sufficient time (e.g., 60 to 90 minutes every other week or weekly) to PLTs as part of the regular daily schedule.
Ensuring accountability to school administrators and each other	Our PLT does not document that our time is used efficiently and is focused on PLT goals (e.g., changing instruction to improve student learning)		Our PLT documents that our time is used efficiently, typically with logs, although we do not have to show progress and there are no major consequences if we do not establish or achieve goals.		Our PLT documents that our time is used efficiently, that our work remains focused, and that we achieve the goals we have set, using logs, action plans, and other tools. There are consequences if we do not document these outcomes.
Allowing teachers to direct efforts	Our PLT work is defined by the goals and approaches of school or district administrators.		Our PLT work is somewhat led by our teachers, in that we define some of our goals, but school or district administrators limit the topics or approaches we can investigate; our work often fits into their requirements.		Our PLT work is led by our teachers, who are encouraged to define our goals based on data and to identify our focus as well as the specific topics, strategies, and approaches we investigate.
Encouraging instructional change	Our school leaders rarely address how teachers change instruction.		Our school leaders sometimes encourage teachers to change instruction, but often in general terms and without giving specific constructive feedback.		Our school leaders regularly encourage teachers to change instruction after observing frequently and providing specific suggestions.
Sharing leadership for decision making	The majority of our school decisions are made autocratically by the principal.		Many of our school decisions are made through collaborative processes involving teachers, but some of the most important decisions are still made primarily by administrators, perhaps with a select few teachers.		Most of our school decisions are based on research and data and are made with all staff willingly participating in collaborative decision-making; consensus is used appropriately.

(2) Our PLT uses student achievement and other types of data to promote student learning.

Components	Level 1	Level 2	Level 3	Level 4	Level 5
Establishing a PLT topic	Our PLT uses little or no student data (e.g., achievement data, classroom data) to establish our PLT focus.		Our PLT uses a limited variety of data (e.g., percent of students meeting standards) to establish our PLT focus.		Our PLT uses a wide variety of data, including student achievement and classroom data, to establish our PLT focus.
Using data to make decisions related to improving student learning	Our PLT uses no data to make decisions and set goals.		Our PLT occasionally uses student achievement and classroom data to make decisions and set goals, although these data are usually school or classroom averages (i.e., not disaggregated).		Our PLT routinely uses student achievement and classroom data disaggregated by individual student and student subgroups, as well as content areas, and over time where possible.
Assessing current classroom (e.g., curricular, instructional, and assessment-related) practices	Our PLT collects little or no data to assess current classroom practice.		Our PLT collects some data on classroom practices, but data tend to be incomplete and are not collected from all teachers.		Our PLT collects classroom practice data systematically (e.g., through surveys, observation checklists, etc.) from all teachers on specified practices.
Monitoring teacher efforts to adapt classroom practices to improve student learning	Our PLT collects little or no data (e.g., classroom assessment results) to determine effects of new/refined practices on student learning.		Our PLT collects some data to determine effects of new practices on student learning, but the data or analyses tend to be incomplete.		Our PLT collects and analyzes sufficient data to reasonably conclude whether the new practices appear likely to positively affect student learning.

(3) Our PLT shares and reflects on classroom practice.

Components	Level 1	Level 2	Level 3	Level 4	Level 5
Reflecting individually on classroom practices to promote student learning	Individual teachers in our PLT rarely reflect on their classroom practices.		Teachers in our PLT sometimes reflect on their classroom practices but usually not deeply.		Teachers in our PLT regularly reflect on their classroom practices through the use of tools and activities that lead to deep-level reflection.
Sharing and reflecting on classroom practices with PLT members to promote student learning	Our PLT rarely shares and reflects on classroom practices together.		Our PLT sometimes shares and reflects on classroom practices together but often in informal discussions (e.g., "hallway talk") between one or two teachers and only sometimes using structured methods to promote greater understanding.		Our PLT regularly shares and reflects on classroom practices together using structured methods (e.g., analyzing student work) that promote continuous improvement and deep reflection on teacher beliefs.
Sharing experiences and student outcomes when first using new or improved classroom practices to promote student learning	Our PLT rarely shares its experiences and student outcomes when using new or improved classroom practices.		Our PLT sometimes shares its experiences and student outcomes when using new or improved classroom practices, but often in informal discussions between one or two teachers and not systematically, as part of their PLT work.		Our PLT members regularly share their experiences and student outcomes related to new or improved classroom practices using structured methods (e.g., analyzing student work) and data collection plans.
Observing in other teachers' classrooms	Teachers in our PLT rarely observe in other teachers' classrooms.		Teachers in our PLT sometimes observe in other teachers' classrooms, usually without meeting in advance to establish common understanding of the lesson or after to debrief and reflect on the lesson.		Teachers in our PLT often observe in other teachers' classrooms, meeting in advance to review lesson goals and purpose of the observation, and afterward to debrief and reflect on the lesson.

(4) Our PLT studies and uses research to improve student learning.

Components	Level 1	Level 2	Level 3	Level 4	Level 5
Reading research and best practices related to PLT topic	Our PLT rarely reads professional journals and research related to our PLT topic.		Our PLT reads professional journals and research related to our PLT topic when asked to.		Our PLT regularly reads professional journals and research related to our PLT topic and shares findings with the team.
Analyzing and evaluating research and best practices related to PLT topic	Our PLT rarely analyzes and evaluates research and best practices related to our PLT topic.		Our PLT sometimes analyzes and evaluates research and best practices related to our PLT topic but mainly when this is required and only occasionally using structured methods that promote deep analysis.		Our PLT regularly analyzes and evaluates research and best practices related to our PLT topic, using tools that promote deep analysis.
Analyzing a variety of research and best practices related to PLT topic	Our PLT does not analyze a variety of research and best practices related to our PLT topic.		Our PLT analyzes informed opinions on best practices and possibly a piece of qualitative or quantitative research related to our PLT topic.		Our PLT regularly analyzes a variety of informed opinions on best practices, as well as qualitative and quantitative research related to our PLT topic. When possible, we review the research cited by the authors of opinion pieces. We include any seminal research related to our PLT topic in discussions.
Using research and best practices to identify new practices to implement (or current practices to refine)	Our PLT rarely identifies new classroom practices to implement (or current practices to refine) based on research and best practices.		Our PLT sometimes identifies new classroom practices to implement (or current practices to refine) based on research and best practices, often without reading sufficiently about the contexts (i.e., students and school) in which these practices have been successful.		Our PLT regularly identifies new classroom practices to implement (or current practices to refine) based on research and best practices with a deep understanding of the contexts in which these practices have been successful.

(5) Our PLT increases its use of research-based classroom practices.

Components	Level 1	Level 2	Level 3	Level 4	Level 5
Using appropriate research-based practices	Our PLT rarely changes classroom practices based on research and best practices.		Our PLT sometimes changes classroom practices, based on research and best practices, but without complete understanding of the contexts in which these practices have been successful.		Our PLT changes classroom practices based on research and best practices with a rich understanding of the contexts in which these practices have been successful.
Improving the quality of classroom practices	Our PLT rarely changes classroom practices with a clear picture of what effective use of the practice looks like.		Our PLT changes classroom practices, often without a clear picture of what effective use of the practice looks like.		Our PLT changes classroom practices based on a clear picture of how to use the practice in our classrooms through activities such as completing an implementation matrix and observing at other schools.
Giving changes in classroom practice sufficient time to work	Our PLT rarely changes classroom practice for more than a brief period of time.		Our PLT changes classroom practices but not over a sufficient period of time (i.e., at least two months) and only sometimes sharing our progress with our PLT.		Our PLT changes classroom practices consistently over at least two months, keeping records we regularly share with our PLT.
Drawing conclusions about strategies and practices	Our PLT rarely draws conclusions about changing classroom practices.		Our PLT draws conclusions about changing classroom practices, but these are not often based on data we collected and do not always represent a consensus view.		Our PLT draws conclusions about changing classroom practice after following a well-documented plan leading to a consensus about next steps around new practices.

(6) Our PLT uses effective collaborative and teamwork skills.

Components	Level 1	Level 2	Level 3	Level 4	Level 5
Using effective team strategies to enhance productivity of PLT efforts	Our PLT rarely uses effective team strategies (e.g., clearly defined team roles, agendas, logs, norms).		Our PLT uses some effective team strategies (e.g., clearly defined team roles, agendas, logs, norms) but not consistently and not always successfully.		Our PLT consistently and successfully uses effective team strategies.
Addressing conflict productively to deepen understanding of differences	Our PLT usually avoids conflict through the use of inappropriate strategies.		Our PLT is beginning to address conflict in appropriate ways.		Our PLT resolves conflict in appropriate ways and to everyone's satisfaction using a collaboratively designed plan.
Communicating clearly and consistently	Our PLT communication is unclear and inconsistent.		Our PLT communication is improving but misunderstandings continue to arise.		Our PLT communication is clear and consistent.
Collaborating on activities	Teachers in our PLT work in isolation.		Some teachers in our PLT collaborate while others work in isolation.		Our PLT collaborates regularly.
Reflecting on team dynamics	Our PLT spends little time reflecting on team dynamics (i.e., how well they are working, learning, and improving practices together).		Our PLT spends some time reflecting on team dynamics but not consistently and without keeping a record of progress.		Our PLT regularly reflects on team dynamics (i.e., how well we are working, learning, and improving practices together) in ways that ensure feedback from all and a record of progress.
Building and maintaining trust	Our PLT lacks trust among individual members, which limits our ability to work together.		Our PLT is making progress in building trust among members, but we still have a way to go.		Our PLT has a high level of trust that contributes to our productivity and ability to work through issues when they come up.
Celebrating successes of PLT to reinforce strengths and lessons learned	Our PLT does not celebrate successes.		Our PLT acknowledges successes but does not usually acknowledge the individuals who made the efforts, measure the gains that have been made, or reflect on lessons learned.		Our PLT regularly reinforces successes by acknowledging individual and group efforts, and by measuring gains and reflecting on lessons learned.

ANTICIPATING POTENTIAL CHALLENGES ■

While we believe the PLT process can be a powerful tool for changing teaching practice to improve student learning, we also know that challenges may come up during implementation. The following section addresses some of those challenges.

How will we find time for training and PLT meetings?

As one school leader said, "The biggest challenge for us is time. When can we get all the teams together to do effective work? That's a challenge everywhere. When you are doing this kind of work, it doesn't lend itself particularly well to one hour a month." However, with sufficient planning, it is possible to carve out time for PLTs to meet. See Chapter 3 and Resource D for information on finding sufficient time for PLTs. It can reduce the effectiveness of PLTs if teachers do not have some paid time within the regular school day to meet. Some schools do provide stipends for teachers' extra time spent on collaborative work.

What do we do about teachers who do not attend training or participate in PLTs?

Many school leaders recognize this as a problem. One administrator points out, "The biggest challenge that I see is the group of teachers, a few teachers in every building, that just don't want to take on anything new or different. Some people do not see the value in this kind of a process because they think that they have done the same thing for 15 years and it works for them. Not everybody is willing to look at data and say, 'Oh, I could do better in this, so what can I do to improve it?' There are some people who are entrenched in their ways and they don't want to change."

Another administrator described a staff composed of mature teachers who had been with the school district for 25 to 30 years. "They had completely lost touch with the educational context outside of their building. They were not aware of reform efforts, of new instructional practices. They were fairly entrenched in their ways. This was an impacted relationship, like an impacted tooth."

In most schools, there are indeed those teachers who resist change, especially if it means altering the way they do things in their own classrooms. It is helpful to get to the root of their resistance. Do they understand how to use data effectively? Is there a personality conflict with others in their team—one that seems insurmountable at the moment? Are they near retirement and just putting in their time until the anticipated end? Is there something going on in their personal life that pulls their time and energy away and makes it difficult to focus on learning something new?

One possible response is to make participation in the PLT process optional for at least the first year. It may be more productive to excuse a couple of recalcitrant individuals from engaging in PLTs while giving them other duties during collaboration time. Another solution is to simply mandate attendance and participation. Each of these options has pros and cons and the individual context must be considered. There is neither a single nor a simple solution to this challenge. It may, however, be helpful to involve the leadership team in working on the response to this issue.

Meeting Resistance

Howard Gardner's book *Changing Minds: The Art and Science of Changing Our Own and Other People's Minds* (2006) provides insight and suggestions for encouraging resisters to halt their resistance and participate. Gardner identifies seven factors that can be used to bring about changes in people's thinking. Think about using some of Gardner's strategies. This may require further reading, leadership team discussion, and some preparation.

1. Reason: appeal to rational thinking. Identify factors relevant to collaboration as well as staff resistance. Working with a group, brainstorm and list all the reasons that support teaming. Then brainstorm the reasons not to team. Look for patterns. Do the pros outweigh the cons? Some things may not receive equal weight. For instance, increased student learning may carry more weight in a school than some of the cons.

2. Research: provide relevant information. Share the research base that supports the idea and effectiveness of teacher collaboration.

3. Resonance: use examples, ideas that appeal to the conscience, the sense of what is morally right and feels right. The purpose of schooling is to educate students and important evidence shows that groups of teachers, working collaboratively can raise student achievement. Is it right to resist something that works to achieve goals? This may require providing evidence from other schools or from teams that are having success in the school.

4. Representational redescription: describe the vision or message in a variety of ways and provide nonthreatening opportunities for people to try on the new idea. Use stories that describe the work and outcomes of effective teams. Use analogies—compare effective teacher collaboration to collaboration in other fields of work. Provide opportunities for teachers to visit schools engaged in collaboration.

5. Resources and rewards: provide incentives. Think about the resources that teams will need (e.g., additional paid time, a place to meet, class coverage for peer observation and coaching, refreshments, space to store materials, extra copies of materials). Will these resources be provided to the entire staff regardless of participation? Or will they be given only to teams engaged in collaboration to support their work?

6. Real world events: use real stories. The literature on teacher learning communities and professional learning communities provides multiple examples from real schools about the power of collaboration.

7. Resistances: understand and challenge the prevailing resistances. Ask questions to understand why those resisting do not want to participate in a team. This may need to be done in private rather than confronting someone in front of a group. Use active listening skills and keep an open mind to the perception of the other person.

Adapted from Howard Gardner (2006, pp. 15–19)

What can we do with changes in leadership at the school?

Some teachers are so accustomed to administrator turnover that they have become jaded. Their response to the vision and directives of new leaders is often, "This too shall pass." Some of these teachers may give the process less than their best effort and engagement, failing to see the value of this type of professional development. They have become accustomed to what some educators term *the flavor of the year* or *drive-by staff development*.

It is important for teachers to understand that the PLT process is intentionally designed to fit with the six features of effective professional development identified in the research and cited in Chapter 1 of this guide. It is also important to engage teachers in the leadership team and to build teacher leadership. For teachers to believe in the process, they need to be involved in making some of the decisions around PLTs. Their support will grow as they begin to see positive changes in student engagement and academic achievement. Once teachers engage in and experience the power of collaboration and its effect on their students and their own professional life, most will want to continue this process as a way of working for the success of their students. If the PLT process becomes embedded in the daily work of teachers, it should continue as the normal way of working within the school, regardless of staff changes.

In their book *Sustainable Leadership*, Hargreaves and Fink (2006) provide insights into maintaining educational change and leadership in ways that are not reliant on the presence of a single administrator. As discussed in Chapter 3, length is the second of seven principles of sustainability. "*Sustainable leadership lasts*. It preserves and advances the most valuable aspects of life over time, year upon year, from one leader to the next" (p. 18). This lies at the heart of educational change, assuring that positive innovation becomes institutionalized, becomes an expected way of doing business in a given school. This means that each successive principal does not come in mandating change for the sake of change. Principals and other leaders consider their legacy when they move on. They work to build capacity among staff, students, and community that will live beyond their tenure at an institution. While there is much more to sustainable leadership, it behooves leaders to consider up front how to sustain a schoolwide structure for teacher collaboration over time.

What can we do if a particular PLT team leader does not believe in the process?

Another administrator reports, "If you have a really good team leader, you are going to have a more successful team. However, if you have a team leader who doesn't have the buy-in, and we have one of those, it obviously makes it much more difficult for the entire team to function productively."

Rotating roles can help circumvent this problem. If all team members have the opportunity to act as facilitator, they get the chance to practice and experience their own leadership skills. They can then view the work of the team from the perspective of a leader. In reality, the growth of teacher leadership is a common and welcome outcome when teachers collaborate.

Some schools, particularly large high schools, choose to use a group of PLT leaders in a *train the trainer* model. Choosing these trainers for their ability to lead, to train, and to support the process is important. Developing a job description for the position of leader or trainer is also important. Involving the leadership team in making decisions about the way training proceeds—and about important characteristics for trainers or PLT leaders—can use the collaborative process to great advantage. See Resource G for a sample description of expectations for a teacher-facilitator.

How can we get teachers to start to locate their own research?

As one principal noted, "If you send them off individually to search for research, they tend to go grade papers or work on their lesson plans. It's really difficult to get teachers to do that research piece." With the many demands on teachers' time, it can be challenging to get them to search out different classroom practices and the research that supports their proposed changes. Initially, it is helpful to provide suggested strategies and some research to PLTs. School librarians can provide a valuable service by locating research on specific topics for teams. After a time, encourage teachers to begin to search out their own resources. They may need training to use an Internet search and library resources to locate and evaluate the usefulness of research. Asking PLTs to share research with the rest of the staff provides some accountability.

> *Continuous learning about relevant research and best practice should be "job embedded" as a regular and expected part of a teacher's responsibilities. Professional learning communities are ideally suited to support this role.*
>
> Jay McTighe, 2008, p. 6

What can we do if some of our teachers resent an outside facilitator coming in?

After working with external facilitators for a year, one middle school chose to respond to this challenge by training a cadre of their own teachers as facilitators for their PLTs. The external facilitator provided training, guidance, and resources to the cadre through regularly scheduled sessions, along with telephone and e-mail support. Local facilitators know the staff and school context, and this can be a productive solution. On the other side, sometimes the school or district can benefit by using a skilled outside facilitator with the perspective and ability to play a key role in developing teacher learning communities (McLaughlin & Talbert, 2006). It is important to make sure facilitators are skilled in leading the PLT process as well as a good fit for the particular school context.

What can we do if teachers reproduce existing cliques as they select into PLTs?

As one principal said, "Staff members need to get past their personal interests and become objective and focused on what is best for student learning and the school." Another principal added, "It is necessary to establish shared values and let that drive the work rather than being part of a team with their friends." Using data to identify student needs and using a PLT selection process that specifies clear criteria for forming teams will help avoid cliques. At times, the principal or a facilitator may need to intervene to shift the focus to "what is best for our students."

What about those staff members who see the PLT process as an add-on?

PLTs are specifically designed to direct teachers to focus on issues that affect their own students' learning. Starting with an in-depth examination of student data early in the year offers a productive avenue for understanding overall learning needs. Coupling this with training and tools to manipulate data to examine the needs, skills, and progress of a specific group of students helps teachers focus on issues that are important to them. This then includes examining their own practice and making necessary changes to reach the goal of improved student achievement. It helps when teachers can readily see that PLT goals are aligned with the school and district improvement goals. Developing teacher leaders as spokespersons and intermediaries can make a difference, too.

It is important to take the necessary time to plan for PLT implementation before beginning. While many schools are under pressure to bring up test scores to meet adequate yearly progress (AYP) requirements, it is essential to be intentional about changes. That requires thoughtful planning as well as rapid movement toward implementing those changes. It is also valuable to reinforce the idea that PLTs are a powerful method for altering school culture in positive ways. Collaboration should not just become a buzzword representing the *flavor of the year*. Instead it can be viewed as a valuable way to work toward the common goal of improving student learning. Schoolwide sharing can provide the *bigger picture*, helping teachers view the PLT work within the framework of the entire system. As with anything new in the workplace, initial training and implementation takes time. This underscores the need to provide regularly scheduled and protected time for teacher collaboration.

What can we do if multiple initiatives in a district compete for teachers' attention and time?

In many schools working to reform, teachers experience an abundance of professional development aimed at getting them to incorporate new strategies into their daily work. Many of these strategies are research based and worthwhile. However, teachers can begin to feel overwhelmed by all the material and information given to them. They may need to choose which strategies to implement with their specific students. The PLT process can serve as an organizing process as they list all the strategies and thoughtfully examine each one; perhaps allowing each PLT to implement one or two separate strategies helps teachers organize and make sense out of this information. Rather than feeling overwhelmed, they can use their PLT to effectively integrate strategies in a sensible way.

The staff in one underperforming school had received training in 16 different areas (Understanding by Design, Smart Goals, to mention a few) in hopes of providing teachers with tools to increase student achievement. PLT facilitators led them through an activity to explore the relevance of each strategy for their specific students. They described each strategy and brainstormed information under the following categories:

- Reasons to adopt this strategy
- Challenges with this strategy
- Actions to take regarding this strategy

In this way they narrowed it down to a manageable set of tools to incorporate into the work of their PLT. Since most strategies were research based, they bypassed consulting the research in order to move directly into implementing and assessing results.

We know that administrators need to sit in on PLT meetings, but other duties frequently pull their attention elsewhere. What can we do?

There are many competing demands on an administrator's time. There is no easy answer to this challenge except to say that it is important for administrators to set aside time to sit in with teams at least once every few weeks. They may rotate among teams to get a sense of the nature of the work and to understand the interpersonal dynamics and instructional focus of each team. Asking teams to report out two to three times a year is necessary but insufficient. Administrator visibility throughout the school, along with interest and support for PLTs, cannot be overemphasized. Administrators need to create conditions to develop teacher leaders, but this does not take the place of their ongoing support, communication, and interaction with each PLT.

ACTION   **Preparing to Meet Potential Challenges**

- Assess the strengths of the staff and prepare to acknowledge them up front.
- List potential challenges that might come up in introducing and implementing PLTs in the school.
- As a team, discuss any potential positive outcomes from these challenges. For example, open discussion of staff objections may bring out something you have not considered.
- For each challenge, brainstorm ways to respond.
- Understand that you may never be prepared for all challenges; acknowledge and celebrate when you have surmounted an obstacle, no matter how small.
- Remember, early work on building and maintaining trust will ease the way when facing challenges.

CELEBRATING SUCCESS ■

Change, while exhilarating, can also be draining. Schools have often been stripped of the symbolic acts that help culture survive and thrive. There is a need to revive ritual and ceremonies as the spiritual fuel that energizes and puts more life back into schools (Deal & Peterson, 1999). Celebration is one of the most important and effective strategies for shaping the culture of any organization. Celebrations help us to do the following:

- Link the past with the present
- Signal what is important in an organization
- Reinforce behaviors and shared values while encouraging others to act in accordance with those values
- Exemplify underlying assumptions
- Supply momentum to continue efforts by providing evidence of short term wins that are critical to sustaining change (DuFour, 1998)

It is important to note the small positive changes as well as to observe significant milestones. The PLT process can be rejuvenating as teachers learn the benefits of working collaboratively. However, teaching requires physical, mental, and emotional involvement with students all day long. PLTs add the dimension of that same involvement with a team of adults in the school community. Celebration doesn't always have to take the form of cheers and kudos. Sometimes quiet reflection on progress—on a job well done—can be a form of celebration.

Celebration can focus on the collective commitments to learning for both students and staff, on nonacademic achievements, and on academic progress. Adult learning can also be celebrated by including "sharing the learning time when teams can share new ideas, products, and insights that have resulted from their collaboration" (Eaker, DuFour, & DuFour, 2002, p. 104). This can take place during regular staff meetings as well as the scheduled whole-school PLT sharing. When planning and scheduling the work of PLTs, it is essential for leaders to intentionally include celebration in those plans.

> *The superintendent and curriculum director attended our year-end presentations. They were certainly impressed. It was a powerful, effective way to encapsulate the whole year.*
>
> Cathy Carson, Principal, St. Helens, Oregon

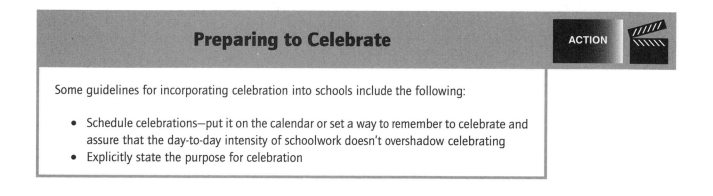

Preparing to Celebrate

ACTION

Some guidelines for incorporating celebration into schools include the following:

- Schedule celebrations—put it on the calendar or set a way to remember to celebrate and assure that the day-to-day intensity of schoolwork doesn't overshadow celebrating
- Explicitly state the purpose for celebration

- Make celebration everyone's responsibility
- Establish a clear link between public recognition and the advancement of vision and values
- Create opportunities for lots of winners
- Acknowledge small achievements as well as the large ones
- Remind individual PLTs to celebrate regularly

■ KEY POINTS FOR CHAPTER 5

Supporting the Work of PLTs

- Leaders and teams need to understand and pay attention to the key factors supporting the success of PLTs.
- Leaders reinforce the importance of the PLT process and strategies by doing the following:
  o Regularly attending PLT trainings
  o Using collaboration skills in meetings and other school activities
  o Reading and sharing research and key points with staff
  o Ensuring that PLTs are teacher led but remaining involved to provide necessary guidance and support

- Leaders can encourage use of the PLT rubric to assist teams in reflection and self-evaluating
- Leaders who anticipate some of the challenges and work with them as they come up during PLT implementation can help ensure more successful outcomes for PLTs
- Celebrate success often—this helps the entire staff notice and appreciate positive changes as well as reinforces the shared vision for school improvement

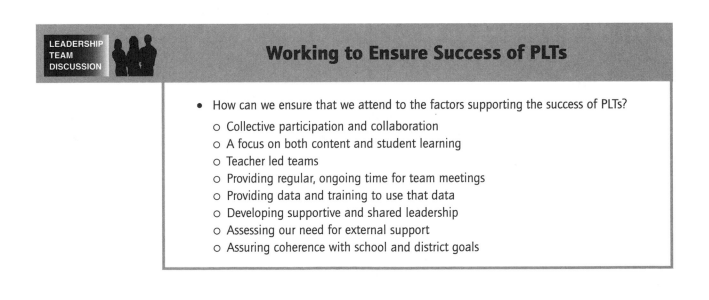

LEADERSHIP TEAM DISCUSSION

Working to Ensure Success of PLTs

- How can we ensure that we attend to the factors supporting the success of PLTs?
  o Collective participation and collaboration
  o A focus on both content and student learning
  o Teacher led teams
  o Providing regular, ongoing time for team meetings
  o Providing data and training to use that data
  o Developing supportive and shared leadership
  o Assessing our need for external support
  o Assuring coherence with school and district goals

- What are the specific ways we will reinforce the PLT process and strategies?
- How do we provide leadership and oversight while assuring that PLTs are led by teachers?
- What potential challenges are likely to occur in this school?
- Are there other challenges that might come up due to our specific school context? How will we work with those challenges?
- How can we use the PLT rubric to assist teams to self-evaluate?
- How can we intentionally and regularly celebrate success?

Notes:

Resources

Resource A

■ NATIONAL STAFF DEVELOPMENT COUNCIL (NSDC) STANDARDS FOR STAFF DEVELOPMENT

Context Standards

Staff development that improves the learning of all students does the following:

- Organizes adults into learning communities whose goals are aligned with those of the school and district.
- Requires skillful school and district leaders who guide continuous instructional improvement.
- Requires resources to support adult learning and collaboration.

Process Standards

Staff development that improves the learning of all students does the following:

- Uses disaggregated student data to determine adult learning priorities, monitor progress, and help sustain continuous improvement.
- Uses multiple sources of information to guide improvement and demonstrate its impact.
- Prepares educators to apply research to decision-making.
- Uses learning strategies appropriate to the intended goal.
- Applies knowledge about human learning and change.
- Provides educators with the knowledge and skills to collaborate.

Content Standards

Staff development that improves the learning of all students does the following:

- Prepares educators to understand and appreciate all students; create safe, orderly and supportive learning environments; and hold high expectations for their academic achievement.
- Deepens educators' content knowledge, provides them with research-based instructional strategies to assist students in meeting rigorous academic standards, and prepares them to use various types of classroom assessments appropriately.
- Provides educators with knowledge and skills to involve families and other stakeholders appropriately. Revised 2001.

SURVEY OF SCHOOL CAPACITY ■
FOR CONTINUOUS IMPROVEMENT

The Survey of School Capacity for Continuous Improvement, formerly the School Readiness for Reform Survey, asks questions about several characteristics of your school that are often areas of concern when school faculties plan reform and improvement efforts. The survey is intended to help your faculty develop a shared understanding of these characteristics in your school, provide a stimulus for frank discussion, and provide a place to start planning for specific reform and improvement activities. The results can help school staff identify the aspects of school climate that will support change and where to focus attention to improve the conditions that foster successful improvement initiatives.

The survey can be accessed at www.nwrel.org/assessment/School Capacity/about.php. There is no charge to the school for completing the survey and receiving school reports. School principals can register to have their staff members complete the survey from the Create Account page. The survey can also be set up on a district level instead of a school level. More information on how to establish an account for this capacity can be found on the Help page.

Survey questions are grouped under the following seven categories:

- Clear School Direction (Mission and Vision)
- Shared Facilitative Leadership
- Staff Collaboration
- Personal Commitment by Teachers
- Challenging Curriculum and Engaged Student Learning
- Communications With Parents, Community Members, and Business Partners
- Meaningful Involvement of Parents, Community Members, and Business Partners

Using Adobe Acrobat Reader, you may review the survey questions, the interpretation guide, and sample school reports online:

- Survey Questions: www.nwrel.org/assessment/SchoolCapacity/School_ Capacity_Question_List.pdf
- Interpretation Guide: www.nwrel.org/assessment/SchoolCapacity/ Interpretation_Guide.pdf
- Sample Reports: www.nwrel.org/assessment/SchoolCapacity/Sample_ Reports.pdf

The sample school reports were created from the combined responses of all teachers who completed the survey from January 2004 to June 2004.

Resource C

■ PROFESSIONAL LEARNING COMMUNITY (PLC) SURVEY

The Professional Learning Community (PLC) survey is a research-based, validated instrument that measures the degree of *professional community* among teachers in a school across six facets. Together, these facets define a professional learning community:

- Organizational learning,
- Collective responsibility,
- Focus on student learning,
- Reflective dialogue,
- Staff collegiality and collaboration, and
- Deprivatized practice.

Research on restructuring schools has shown that these facets of teacher professional community have significant positive effects on student achievement. The instrument is especially useful in stimulating discussion among staff looking to develop greater professional community.

The survey can be accessed at the following Web site:

http://www.nwrel.org/csdi/services/plt/PLCSurvey/

Using Adobe Acrobat Reader, you may review the survey questions and sample school reports online:

- Survey Questions: http://www.nwrel.org/csdi/services/plt/PLCSurvey/PLC_Question_List.pdf
- Sample report: http://www.nwrel.org/csdi/services/ plt/PLCSurvey/PLC_Sample_Report.pdf

Resource D

FINDING TIME FOR PROFESSIONAL LEARNING ■

Compiled by Jennifer L. Jensen,
Northwest Regional Educational Laboratory

Professional learning teams (PLTs), focused on improving student success, need dedicated time together that is regular, consistent, and sustained over the long term. This time for learning and collaboration must be built into the regular school day (Lewis, 2000). Teacher learning alone will not improve student learning. Teachers need the time to acquire new ideas, experiment in their classrooms, collect data on the changes they are making, and share results with colleagues (Garet, Birman, Porter, Desimone, & Herman, with Yoon, 2001; Smylie, Allensworth, Greenberg, Harris, & Luppescu, 2001).

There are a number of different strategies for finding time. Most of the examples detailed in this section are from schools that used just one method; however, a combination might be employed to provide every staff member with the opportunity to participate in a PLT. Some staff members might have substitutes cover their classes during the school day, while others choose to meet on their own time in return for making formal inservice days voluntary rather than mandatory. Still others might prefer to take advantage of a flex-time schedule. The key to implementing a menu of team opportunities successfully is to provide staff members with a choice; their participation may be mandatory, but how they choose to participate should not be mandated unless there is staff consensus on one clearly advantageous method.

STRATEGY I: ELIMINATE ■

Duty Periods

Many teachers spend an entire class period, from 50 to 90 minutes in a given day, on supervisory tasks unrelated to actual teaching. Schools that do not have duty periods within the school day may still involve their teachers in such work before and after classes. There is no professional reason for teachers to spend time as hall monitors, lunchroom supervisors, or playground police (Maeroff, 1993; Sparks & Hirsch, 2000). Time for professional learning and collaboration may be found by examining duty requirements with an informed and critical eye.

- Identify which duties are essential and determine whether state or district requirements are suggested guidelines or non-negotiable mandates.
- If allowed by law, find parent or retired community volunteers to relieve or supplement certified staff during duty periods, or hire part-time workers.

Traditional Inservice Days

Most schools build a number of full or half days into the school calendar for teacher inservice education. These days are distinct from planning or work days, which assist teachers to get ready for a new school year or to complete students' grades at the end of a grading period or school year. They are also distinct from work days in their productivity: Traditional inservice opportunities produce little to no effect on teachers' practice in their classrooms. While isolated days sprinkled sparsely throughout the year will not support effective teaming either, these hours can be redistributed into regular, ongoing time for teams. Many states or districts will grant waivers to the required inservice schedule for schools that document how a comparable amount of time will be used for other types of professional learning.

If the traditional inservice calendar must be maintained, consider making attendance on some or all of these days optional for staff that volunteer regular ongoing team-meeting time outside the contract day and document their participation.

At Mission Bay High School in San Diego, California, teachers "chose to select for themselves when their study groups would meet each week. The groups met at different times and on different days. Several of the 17 study groups met early in the morning, others at lunch time or during planning periods, others after school, and one met in the evening. Teachers accounted for their professional development time and, on designated staff development days, teachers were not expected to attend meetings" (Murphy, 1997, p. 31).

Faculty Meetings

Similarly, faculty meetings in most schools do not use professional time efficiently. If faculty meetings concern mostly administrative matters, which could just as easily be handled by e-mail or memo, reduce their frequency or eliminate them altogether. Staff members will learn to look for electronic or paper announcements.

If meeting time has been an hour or more, shift this time directly to teams. If faculty meetings have been of shorter duration, *bank* the time by allowing teachers to arrive late or leave early on some former meeting days in return for arriving early or staying past their contract time on others or use the time to supplement hours gained from reallocating some or all of scheduled inservice days.

At Deepwood Elementary School in Round Rock, Texas, "the principal limits faculty meetings to one Wednesday a month. Study groups meet on the other three Wednesdays of the month. All teachers in the district are asked to reserve every Wednesday for faculty meetings" (Murphy & Lick, 1998, p. 63).

Other Activities

Scrutinize the existing school schedule and budget for activities that do not directly contribute to student achievement or staff professional learning. "Invite a variety of individuals to search [for these days] . . . . [M]ultiple perspectives can often find possibilities that have been overlooked" and bear in mind that often resources such as time and money are allocated to activities "simply because they always have been" (Pankake, 1998, p. 144). Funds freed from less-productive activities can be used for substitutes or extended contract hours for some teams; other teams can be organized around the time found.

In one example, cited by Morrissey and Cowan (2000), a principal scheduled "evening meetings to share information with the staff, often providing dinner, or asking teachers to potluck. This ensured the regularly scheduled during- and after-school time would be free for collaboration, rather than taken up by administrative meetings" (p. 20).

STRATEGY 2: EXTENDED LUNCH ■

In schools with a single common lunch period for all students, this time can be extended once a week or every other week to provide time for staff teams to meet. If allowed by state law, parent or community volunteers can supervise students and conduct that day's activity. If not, substitute teachers can be hired. Responsibility for planning the activity can be shared in rotation among the teams meeting during the extended lunch. Activities and supervision could be planned for the student body as a whole or in grade-level groups.

At Kendon Elementary School in Lansing, Michigan, the lunch period for teachers is extended to twice its normal length every other Friday. This means that for 80 minutes, the teachers are able to have the kind of concentrated, duty-free time together that those who work in elementary schools seldom get. Typically, a portion of the time is given over to a whole faculty activity and the other half to meeting in teams or small groups. This opportunity comes on top of the half-day a week that is available to teachers for meetings of study groups.

> Meanwhile, the school's 300 students—except the kindergartners, whose school day ends at the start of lunch—spend the time eating, playing at recess, and attending an activity with educational content. The educational activity is held twice during the teachers' extended lunch so that half of the students can be at recess while the rest attend the activity. . . . Aides are hired specifically to come to the school during the extended lunch to be with the children. Having the students eat in their classrooms with the aides helps minimize rowdiness. (Maeroff, 1993, p. 125)

Kendon also cites challenges with keeping students productively engaged during this period, which they have countered by expecting teachers to set a context for the Friday lesson during regular class time and follow-up afterwards.

STRATEGY 3: FLEX TIME ■

Flex time allows teachers to arrive at school at different times and adjust the time they leave according to the daily hours mandated by their contracts. For some schools, this method can create an adequate length of time, either before or after school, for teams of teachers on the same flex schedule to meet for collegial learning. For example, if teachers are required to arrive at school

30 minutes before students and stay 45 minutes after, teachers who flexed their time to arrive 15 minutes before students and stay for one hour after would have an hour available for a team meeting after school every day. Others could arrive and leave earlier for before-school team meetings.

Flex time can also be implemented only on those days when meetings are scheduled. These can be scheduled around duty requirements to ensure that student supervision is not negatively affected.

Broadmoor Junior High School in Pekin, Illinois, "allows teachers three options for their workday: 7:15–3:00, 7:30–3:15, or 7:45–3:30, with the understanding that they must attend scheduled faculty meetings" (Hackmann & Berry, 2000, p. 47).

At Brushy Creek Elementary School in Round Rock, Texas, "the principal makes allowances for the time teachers spend after school in their study groups. If teachers are expected to stay 45 minutes after students are dismissed and a group of teachers in a study group stays an hour and half beyond dismissal time, those teachers will be allowed to leave earlier than the 45 minutes on the other days of the week" (Murphy, 1997, p. 31).

■ STRATEGY 4: HIRING SUBSTITUTE TEACHERS OR ADMINISTRATIVE SUBSTITUTES

Hiring substitute teachers can be a very productive method for releasing teams of classroom teachers for professional learning and collaboration during their regular workday. It presents some obvious challenges, the same ones faced by a teacher who is absent for any other reason: Planning for the substitute often requires substantial time, continuity of learning can be interrupted for *subproof* lesson plans, and the quality—as well as the content—of instruction may suffer.

These challenges can be alleviated somewhat through hiring a regular team of substitutes who step in for the same teachers during regular meeting times. For example, if a school had a four-period block schedule, one class period would be sufficient for a weekly team meeting. If the school had 10 five-member PLTs, five substitutes would be hired for 2.5 days per week. The same substitute would replace the same teacher during the same period every week. Because these substitutes spend several days per week in the school, they are available to coordinate with teachers prior to the class periods and their familiarity with students reduces behavior problems.

In a school with sufficient administrative and counseling staff, a team of administrators and/or counselors can step in to substitute for one or more teams of teachers each week while they engage in professional learning. Not only is this method less expensive, but it also provides these staff members with an opportunity to get to know students in a different context than their usual interactions, while also helping them keep in touch with the realities of teaching in today's classrooms.

Broadmoor Junior High School employs permanent substitute teachers. "One of their responsibilities is to substitute for teachers engaged in collaborative planning. Teachers are more comfortable leaving their classrooms in the care of staff members who know their students, understand the teachers' class expectations, and can continue meaningful class instruction in the teachers' absence" (Hackmann & Berry, 2000, p. 47).

Holmes Middle School in Flint, Michigan, tried hiring substitute teachers, but regular classroom teachers "found themselves returning to their classrooms with a sense of dread. The substitutes were little more than strangers walking through an unfamiliar neighborhood, and the students acted out every mischievous and aggressive fantasy they ever harbored." Rather than give up, they tried a new approach: "Three resource teachers were hired as, in effect, regular substitutes for teachers who received reallocated time. No longer would as many teachers be released at once, but those who were away from their classrooms did not have to pay for their absence with a guilty conscience. The same resource teacher showed up in the same classroom each week at the same time; she got to know the students and they got to know her. Furthermore, there was ongoing contact between the resource teacher and the regular teacher to try to make the instructional transition as smooth as possible" (Maeroff, 1993, p. 128).

Sarah Cobb Elementary School in Americus, Georgia, offers another strategy:

Before getting a waiver from the Georgia Board of Education for early release, the Sarah Cobb Elementary School faculty designed a plan to use teaching assistants to release teachers for their study group meetings. The key points of that plan included the following:

- A team of five teaching assistants released five teachers the first hour of school so teachers could meet as a study group.
- For the last hour of school, the teaching assistants covered five other classrooms.
- Each day, two study groups meet. By Friday afternoon, all 10 study groups have met.
- Each week, the groups rotate the time of day they meet. The groups that met the first hour one week would meet the last hour the next week.

Activating this plan the first week of school and continuing it until the waiver was approved in January indicated to the community and the Georgia Board of Education that the faculty was serious about its intent to create a new approach to professional development. (Murphy, 1997, p. 30)

Murphy (1997) also describes the approach taken by Addison Elementary School in Marietta, Georgia:

The principal . . . found a way to enable as many as six study groups to meet in a single day. The principal hired five substitutes who spend one day every other week at the school. On that day, this team of substitutes releases five teachers at 9 a.m. to meet as a study group. The subs release five other teachers at 10 a.m. to meet as a study group, five more at 11 a.m., and so on until the school day ends. Because the school has 10 study groups, the team returns the next day for a half-day to enable the other four study groups to meet. During the weeks in which substitutes don't provide the released time, the study groups meet for an hour after school. (p. 30)

■ STRATEGY 5: EARLY DISMISSAL OR LATE ARRIVAL FOR STUDENTS

An early dismissal or late arrival does not have to be accompanied by a loss of instructional time. Schools find various ways to account for the hours during which students are absent from school: lengthening the other school days, creating service learning requirements, or offering students school-to-work internships.

Lengthening the normal school day requires parental and district support due to the child care and bus schedule changes that accompany it. Waivers from the state and/or district for early dismissal or late arrival schedules are usually readily obtained as long as the school can demonstrate that it will retain minimum requirements for instructional time. The staff will also need to have this change approved through their unions in districts with collective bargaining, as well as reach consensus that they can support this change themselves.

A late arrival has two distinct advantages over an early dismissal. An early dismissal can interfere with afternoon school activities, such as sports practices and games, unless provision is made for students who must remain at school between dismissal and the activity while all staff are involved in professional learning. This problem usually is not encountered in schools with a late arrival or with service learning or internship programs, because students are transported back to the school at the regular dismissal time. Also, late arrival time "may be more effectively used" than an early dismissal "since teachers are not asked to engage in collaborative activities after several hours of instruction" (Hackmann & Berry, 2000, p. 46). Despite the disadvantages, many schools employ an early dismissal with great success.

One key to success is to schedule the early dismissal or late arrival weekly so that "teachers, parents, and students become accustomed to routine deviations from the normal school day" (Hackmann & Berry, 2000, p. 46). It is much easier for stakeholders to remember that every Wednesday is a late arrival day and plan accordingly, than for them to have to count off every other week on a calendar further complicated by school vacations or closures due to weather. A published and widely distributed and promoted school calendar may be of assistance to schools that are unable to schedule weekly time, but arrangements should be made for the larger numbers of students who will forget about the change in schedule.

An example of a school with early dismissal is R.B. Hunt Elementary School, St. Augustine, Florida. This school "uses weekly early-release days for professional development. Administrators requested a waiver from the St. Johns County School District to put their plans for early release in place. Then they developed a schedule for their early release days. In formulating their plan, they considered parental concerns about child care on these days. They sent a memo to all parents asking them to confirm arrangements for their children" (Cook & Fine, 1997).

The following are examples of schools with late arrival.

Brandon and Oxford Professional Development Schools, Ortonville, Michigan

With contributions from all partners, Brandon School District started the PDS [professional development school] in September 1992 and Oxford instituted its program in January 1993. Both restructured the school week to provide two-and-one-half hours each Wednesday morning for staff planning. Each day was lengthened to provide the same or more instructional time.

Under the redesigned school schedule the teacher workday from Monday to Friday is 7:20 a.m. to 2:50 p.m. On Wednesdays, the time from 7:20 a.m. to 10:45 a.m. is used for both professional development time and teacher planning time; students do not report until 11:10 a.m. Teacher lunch lasts until 11:10 a.m., so that the student day begins at 11:10 a.m. Morning and afternoon classes are alternated on a weekly basis, and six minutes are added to each period. (Fulford & Dieterle, 1994)

Holtville High School, Holtville, California

Classes begin 30 minutes late on Wednesdays at Holtville High School. . . . But on Wednesdays, teachers arrive 30 minutes earlier than on the other four days. This gives teachers one hour for collaborative planning in their study groups. (Murphy, 1997, p. 30)

Sweetwater High School, National City, California

At Sweetwater High School in National City, California, a large faculty of 120 teachers found one hour a week for heterogeneous study groups. After analyzing the number of instructional minutes in a regular school day, they determined that the school was "banking" time in terms of instructional minutes. In order to have time in the school day for 20 study groups to meet, they took the accumulated five minutes and combined them with the time from a staff development day to create 26 days when classes could begin 45 minutes later.

Once a week, study groups meet from 7:30 a.m. to 8:15 a.m. On that day, classes begin at 8:20 a.m., and all periods are shortened. On the other four days, classes begin at 7:30 a.m. Students know that on "Study Group Day," the bell schedule is not the same as on the other four days. (Murphy, 1997, p. 31)

STRATEGY 6: SPECIAL STUDIES DAY OR TIME ■

This strategy can create a full day of planning and professional time each week by rearranging students' schedules so that all of the students for one team of teachers devote one entire day to studies with their specialist teachers such as art, music, physical education, and computer sciences. One team's students rotate through these areas on one day, and another team's the next.

A similar technique can be used to create blocks of time throughout the week: Instead of a full day with specialists, that time is divided during several days. At any given period during the week, all of the students of one team of teachers work and learn with one of the specialists available in the building. This variation may work more easily than the full-day method in schools that share specialists with other buildings. In turn, the art, music, physical education, and computer science teachers in either example have a common student-free time to work together as a team.

Although this strategy may seem a more natural fit to elementary schools, where students' schedules are almost identical to those of their classmates, it has also been successfully used in New York City's alternative high schools (Raywid, 1993, p. 32).

One advantage of both of these methods is that they use resources already present in the building, avoiding the expense, as well as the other challenges, of substitute teachers. In addition, neither requires a change in the overall school or bus schedule.

A third variation of this strategy employs college students who function as substitute teachers but are paid in tuition dollars:

> Winnona Park Elementary in Decatur, Georgia, benefits from a team of 19 college students that spend every Thursday at the school. The young men and women are participating in Eco Watch, an environmental leadership program of the Atlanta Outward Bound Center. The college students do classroom and schoolwide environmental activities with the elementary students. This frees teachers to meet in study groups on Thursdays. The college students keep a record of the hours they spend at the school and, at the end of the schoolyear, the hours are converted into dollars for college tuitions. (Murphy, 1997, p. 31)

Your state and district policies regarding the qualifications and certification requirements for adults who supervise students should be thoroughly investigated before considering this variation.

The following is an example of the special studies approach.

Hefferan (West Garfield Park) Elementary School, Chicago, Illinois

> Hefferan has built large blocks of training and planning time into the teachers' schedules in the workplace, during school hours. Teachers are treated as professionals. Parents' talents and those of community volunteers are used to support the work of the school . . . . The staff and the [site council] devised a plan that frees all teachers' time one day a week for team planning and study. As a result, new kinds of teaching and experimentation are taking place, students are enjoying a variety of new experiences, teacher morale and attendance are high, and parent involvement is steadily rising.

Students at Hefferan have four intense days of classroom work each week and a fifth day called *Resource Day*. On Resource Day, students are involved in art, music, gym, library, and computer lab. The students look forward to Resource Days because of the variety in their schedules and the possibilities for creative and experiential learning experiences. With the faculty divided into five instructional teams, each teacher has one free day per week—the Resource Day for students is a planning and study day for teachers. The Resource Day also is economical since no substitute teacher pay is needed. Students simply rotate their classes. Security monitors and parent volunteers are present throughout the building to oversee the rotations from class to class. (Fulford & Dieterle, 1994, p.1)

STRATEGY 7: FOUR-DAY STUDENT WEEK ■

Many schools that have opted for a four-day student week have done so to save money. Only after the budgetary measure was implemented did they discover the many advantages the schedule offers in addition to reduced busing, cafeteria, and custodial costs. As long as all or part of Friday or Monday is maintained in teacher contracts, the most pertinent benefit is regular, ongoing, job-embedded time of sufficient frequency and duration for professional learning teams to thrive.

If the contract hours are cost prohibitive even given other savings or refused by the local union, teams can still volunteer to meet on the open day when they are better rested and have fewer personal obligations than after school, evenings, or weekends. In this situation, ending the work day when students leave two afternoons a week or excusing teachers from formal inservice days might be adequate compensation to make this a permanent solution.

A four-day week does not require that students lose instructional time. Schools lengthen each day so that student-teacher contact time is maintained; state achievement test scores remain stable. Student and teacher morale and attendance improve, while disciplinary referrals and drop-out rates decrease (Fager, 1997). Furthermore, a four-day schedule can allow schools otherwise faced with reducing music, art, sports programs, or other vulnerable activities to find sufficient resources to preserve all or most of these critical offerings.

Examples of schools that have a four-day student week include the following:

Cove School District, Cove, Oregon

Thirteen years ago, Cove School District in rural Northeast Oregon, shifted to a four-day week in response to reduced funding and low student enrollment. The schedule has worked very well for students, teachers, and the community.

Students in grades kindergarten–12 attend school Monday through Thursday from 8 a.m. to 4 p.m., with the last 30 minutes reserved for meetings, clubs, and other activities. Primary students are released at 3 p.m. By reducing lunchtime and the time spent between classes, Cove students spend as much time in school as when they attended five days a week.

Along with the financial savings, there are numerous other benefits associated with the four-day schedule. Because Fridays can be used for athletic events and other school-related activities, there are fewer interruptions in learning Monday through Thursday. Teachers also can use Fridays as an extra work day. Many teachers can be found at school on Friday planning lessons, conducting meetings, or working on other classroom projects.

In the years since its inception in Cove, the four-day school week has been widely accepted by all local education stakeholders. Instead of making student services and activities the target of education cutbacks, the schedule has enabled this small community to continue to provide students with a quality education, full of opportunity and challenge. (Fager, 1997)

George B. White Elementary School, Deerfield, New Hampshire

The students at George B. White

attend school Monday through Thursday from 8:00 to 3:30, instead of Monday through Friday from 8:45 to 2:35. In the four-day week, they get just as many hours of instruction (slightly more, actually).

The faculty, the community, and the New Hampshire Department of Education approved the four-day week for one experimental year. . . . A contingency plan permitted the return to a five-day schedule if the innovation proved too difficult—for example, if younger students got too tired trying to make it through four seven-and-a-half hour days. In fact, however, the Deerfield school . . . still operates on a four-day week 10 years later.

Teachers reserve one Friday a month for schoolwide inservice, sometimes bringing in outsiders to help them rethink some aspect of their practice and sometimes drawing on internal resources. Teachers use other time for such activities as looking at student work in teams and observing classrooms in other schools. Deerfield reports improved student and teacher attendance and morale, as well as higher student energy and motivation. (Featherstone, 1991, p. 28)

■ STRATEGY 8: BLOCK AND MODIFIED-BLOCK SCHEDULES

Block and modified-block schedules exist in many variations but all share one common characteristic: They create longer periods of instructional time for students and teachers. In a 4x4 or alternating block schedule, all instructional time is blocked. Students either take four semester-long classes or eight year-long ones that meet every other day. Blocks are normally about 90 minutes long and a fully blocked day will contain four periods.

However, block schedules can be constructed as creatively as any other kind of school schedule: "Farmington (Missouri) High School adopted a 10-block alternating day schedule that did not meet Missouri's required number of instructional minutes for awarding a Carnegie unit of credit. The faculty and administration readily obtained state approval for their new scheduling approach by increasing the minimum number of credits required for graduation" (Hackmann & Berry, 2000, p. 46). In common modified-block schedules, part of each day is blocked while the balance is composed of traditional 45- to 55-minute periods, or two entire days per week are blocked and the other three maintain a traditional six-, seven-, or eight-period day. In other schools, students take only two classes at a time for 60 days before moving on to the next two.

Block and modified-block schedules are proving to hold many benefits for students and teachers. The longer periods provide time for more in-depth student learning of subject matter and better accommodate the varied rate at which students learn. Students are exposed to a wider variety of instructional methods, including newer, more innovative ones that actively engage students in their own learning and require more time to implement. Textbooks are used less frequently, attendance improves, and failure rates decrease. Students either have longer to prepare for a class, if it meets every other day, or they have fewer classes for which to prepare (Fager, 1997).

One significant benefit of a block schedule is the potential to provide teachers with extended planning and collegial time. If every teacher has 90 minutes a day for planning as a result of block scheduling, a team may more easily choose to devote one planning period per week to professional learning. If students are scheduled into four periods per day rather than eight, arranging common team-planning periods or providing professional learning time through special studies for students is simplified. The pace of a blocked day— one to three class changes rather than five or more—feels less frenetic and leaves teachers better prepared to engage in after-school learning.

However, moving to a block schedule should be approached with caution. Doubling the length of a period requires teachers to expand their repertoire of instructional strategies and carefully choose those that provide appropriate pacing for the period. Before teachers learn *how* to use the time, they must learn *why* a block schedule is desirable. Also, the staff must reach consensus to adopt block scheduling. Planning to successfully implement block scheduling may take one or more years as an appropriate schedule is designed and teachers develop ways to maximize the potential benefit to student learning.

Examples of schools that have adopted block schedules include the following:

Eggers Middle School, Hammond, Indiana

The classic block schedule is used. For teachers, this means daily back-to-back periods—a total of 90 minutes—during which a team of about 10 members can meet. The faculty is divided into three such teams with about 270 children in each of the learning communities for which a team is responsible.

The first of two successive 45-minute segments is typically designated as community planning time. It is a period during which the team discusses such matters as interdisciplinary teaching, thematic units, and individual students. Usually, the second 45 minutes is devoted to individual planning. There is, however, flexibility that allows the team to divide up the 90 minutes each day as it sees fit.

Where are the children during the hour and a half that they are not with their teachers in their learning community? . . . The students spend this time in such ancillary courses as music, art, home economics, industrial arts, computer literacy, and physical education. This is what makes it possible to free the teachers who are teaching the main academic subjects in the interdisciplinary team program . . . . Eggers is different from [some middle schools using this approach] in that students are sent to the ancillary courses each day, which allows daily team gatherings. (Maeroff, 1993, p. 130)

La Grande High School, La Grande, Oregon

This school has a unique block schedule that meets the needs of students, teachers, and the community. "The schedule consists of four 88-minute block periods, and a 58-minute lunch period. Teachers instruct three classes per day and use the remaining 88-minute block for preparation work. Students complete classes in one semester that in previous years would have taken them an entire year. In general, schedules for each student are balanced to provide them with both electives and more academically rigorous classes . . . allow[ing] students to make the most of band, choir, and orchestra throughout the year, while maintaining the structure of the block" (Fager, 1997).

An extensive study of the schedule changes at La Grande was conducted during the 1995–1996 school year by the Eastern Oregon State College Regional Services Institute. The study, which included surveys, interviews, and focus group discussions, showed that the majority of students, former students, teachers, and parents support the block schedule and the other schedule-related changes the school has implemented. Student grade point averages have gone up, while disciplinary referrals have gone down. Teachers who once relied on basic lecture techniques to deliver lessons have become innovative facilitators of learning—continually challenging themselves and their students.

■ STRATEGY 9: BLENDING OPTIONS

Some schools provide multiple meeting times for all of their teachers by combining various methods of finding or creating time. Best Practices High School in Chicago, Illinois, maximizes the quantity and quality of both collegial time for staff and contact time for students through a combination of several of the methods examined separately elsewhere in this resource. Daniels, Bizar, and Zemelman (2001) reported on the school's approach:

One goal of our schedule was to provide ample teacher planning time, and one of the wonderful side effects of our Wednesday internship program (which we stole unabashedly from Central Park East) is a full half day of planning time for teachers every week. An off-campus service learning program has to be the greatest win-win discovery in the history of secondary education: the kids get a powerful, often life-changing experience, while teachers get a half-day of precious collegial time together. Our whole faculty also meets every Monday after school, around 3:15 p.m., with the intention (not always fulfilled) of taking care of our administrative and busywork at that session, leaving the "big stuff"— matters of curriculum and instruction—for the longer Wednesday sessions. We also get some more half-days by using an arcane, Chicago-specific practice called *time-banking*. If you schedule an extra-long school day, you can save up additional minutes and use them to dismiss kids at noon about 18 times a year. In addition to meetings, we schedule teachers so that they have lunch every day with their grade-level team and have their planning period with their department colleagues. With all these structures in place, BPHS teachers probably enjoy better planning and professional development time than faculty at most other high schools—though it never, ever seems like enough. And even though our teachers have lots of time with colleagues, they still spend more time in class than regular Chicago teachers. In fact, to make the schedule legal, our faculty must vote to approve a waiver of local union rules each year. (Daniels et al., 2001, pp. 177–178)

Resource E

■ RESOLVING CONFLICT: KEY TO COLLABORATION

Stephanie Hirsh

Staff development that improves the learning of all students provides educators with the knowledge and skills to collaborate.

When schools try serious restructuring, problems are inevitable. The more ambitious the change that is sought, the more problems that may arise. In order to accomplish significant change, schools must be able to successfully manage their problems.

Embedded in NSDC's standard on collaboration is a concept that groups must learn to manage the conflict that inevitably arises when participants discuss fundamental beliefs about teaching and learning and seek the best ways to improve student achievement.

Working together every day and coming to joint decisions about what will be taught and how it will be taught can be very challenging. And if teachers are expected to come to consensus on what will be taught and how it will be taught, most will presume that everything will not go their way and anticipate differences of opinion that could lead to conflict. Most people fear conflict and take steps to avoid it.

Here's a simple conflict resolution strategy that works.

1. Clarify the problem. Ensure everyone understands what they are arguing about. Write it down. Get agreement on it.

2. Separate positions from interests. Clarify individuals' interests. Interests are characterized by an individual's needs, desires, or fears. Position is represented by a solution to the problem—key words that may trigger someone who is discussing her position are *more*, *less*, or *get*. Focus on interests and indicate that solutions will be addressed later.

3. Identify criteria for a win-win resolution. Seek answers to these questions: What must the outcome achieve? What will an acceptable resolution accomplish? Look at the interests to provide criteria for the resolution. List criteria for solutions that will be acceptable to all parties.

4. Brainstorm potential solutions without judgments. List solutions as they are suggested.

5. Evaluate each solution against the criteria. Craft a matrix to see which solution meets the most criteria.

6. If more than one solution meets all the criteria, then discuss which solution to accept. Choose the best solution.

Consider the process in the following situation. The first- and fourth-grade teams were resisting a proposed change in the scheduling of special-area teachers (art, music, physical education). While each team had a desirable schedule *position* in mind, the facilitator first identified their interests. First grade wanted a two-hour time block for uninterrupted reading instruction and preferably in the morning. Fourth grade was taking advantage of special areas next to lunch to create two hours for team planning and wanted to continue that. Several options were explored. Various special area schedules were brainstormed. Before and after school suggestions for team meetings were posted. Varying the reading instruction schedule was also offered. Each was posted and later judged according to the criteria. Ultimately, the teams found a solution that met everyone's criteria and didn't disrupt anyone else's schedule.

By embracing conflict as an opportunity to pursue better solutions, you'll be closer to arriving at the new vision for professional learning advocated by NSDC and closer to convincing colleagues that daily collegial learning is essential for advancing the performance of every teacher and student.

Source: Hirsh, S. (2003, March). Resolving conflicts key to collaboration. *Results*. Oxford, OH: National Staff Development Council. Retrieved May 5, 2009, from http://www.nsdc.org/news/results/res3-03hirs.cfm

Resource F

■ SAMPLE CONFLICT SCENARIOS

Scenario 1

Your team has six members. Five of you work very well together, contribute ideas to the team, and offer to gather materials, resources, and some research on your chosen topic. The sixth member skips meetings occasionally, comes late to most meetings that he does attend, and rarely speaks or participates in a meaningful way. Two of you have talked about this and are really irritated. You want him to become a fully participating member of the team. You feel disrespected by his lack of interest and participation. At one point, one of you confronted him about this behavior and his response was, "I can spend this time more effectively working in my own classroom alone."

Scenario 2

Your team has four members. In most of your team discussions, one member dominates the conversation. She does have a lot of experience and knowledge, but the meetings tend to focus on her agenda, and at times seem like a one-woman show. As a result, two of the members withdraw from discussions. They take notes and appear to participate by listening, but they rarely offer opinions or contribute new ideas. You know that one of them, a new young teacher, is taking a class on adolescent literacy and has important new information to contribute. In passing his room, you observe that students are deeply engaged in activities. However, this teacher seems intimidated and afraid to offer new ideas.

Scenario 3

There seems to be a personality conflict between some members of your seven-member team. One member doesn't get along with two of the other members. You have heard rumors about arguments between these teachers in the past, but you have not witnessed anything yourself. However, the negative vibe between these people is apparent to everyone on the team and detracts from the cohesion of the PLT. In fact, there are often subtle comments that indicate real animosity between them.

Scenario 4

Your five-member team was working together very well, focusing on using some specific literacy strategies to improve reading comprehension skills. One member takes a two-month leave for health reasons, and her long-term substitute joins your team. On occasional, he comes late to meetings, and several times has stepped out to take a cell phone call during a meeting. He sometimes brings student assignments to grade during meetings. This is not only distracting when it happens, but you feel that the focus and work of the entire team is diminishing.

Resource G

POSSIBLE EXPECTATIONS FOR ■ PLT TEAM LEADERS AND FACILITATORS

Some schools choose to train a cadre of teachers as PLT team leaders or liaisons. These individuals, in turn, train their colleagues and help oversee PLT implementation. We recommend that schools ensure that these leaders understand ahead of time the commitment they are making to work with their colleagues. These leaders will conduct training and model leadership and facilitation. Ideally, each PLT will have one of these leaders as a member.

PLT facilitators are expected to do the following:

- Attend all PLT trainer of trainers sessions
- Plan and deliver subsequent training to their colleagues
- Assure that the PLT tools and processes are a good fit for the context of the school and their specific PLT
- Develop their leadership skills as they work with peers and be willing to share leadership with peers
- Engage colleagues in learning-centered conversations
- Communicate with the school leadership about progress and team needs
- Assist their PLT in preparing presentations to document PLT work—chosen strategies, methods of assessment, results, and recommendations
- Qualifications for PLT liaisons include the following traits:

  ○ Communication and relationship skills that support working with peers
  ○ Willingness to develop their own leadership skills and those of team members
  ○ Ability to contribute to the development of trust among the school community
  ○ Content-area knowledge

Resource H

TOOLS

This section contains masters of the following tools that appear throughout the guide:

1. Professional Learning Team Inquiry Cycle

2. PLT Inquiry Cycle With Steps Explained

3. Getting Started: Sample Agenda for Workshop 1

4. PLT Team Log Form

5. Sample PLT Team Meeting Agenda and Log

6. Defining Team Roles

7. Professional Learning Team: Planning Sheet

8. Five Dimensions of Professional Learning Communities

9. Criteria for Quality Team Time

10. Finding Time for Collaboration

11. Factors Supporting the Success of PLTs

12. PLT Implementation Rubric

13. Getting Started Roadmap

The masters can be used in presentations to faculty, parents, community members, district office personnel, and school board members. The masters are suitable for the following:

- Creating overhead transparencies
- Inserting into PowerPoint presentations
- Duplicating for handouts
- Enlarging for use as posters

Tool H-1   Professional Learning Team Inquiry Cycle

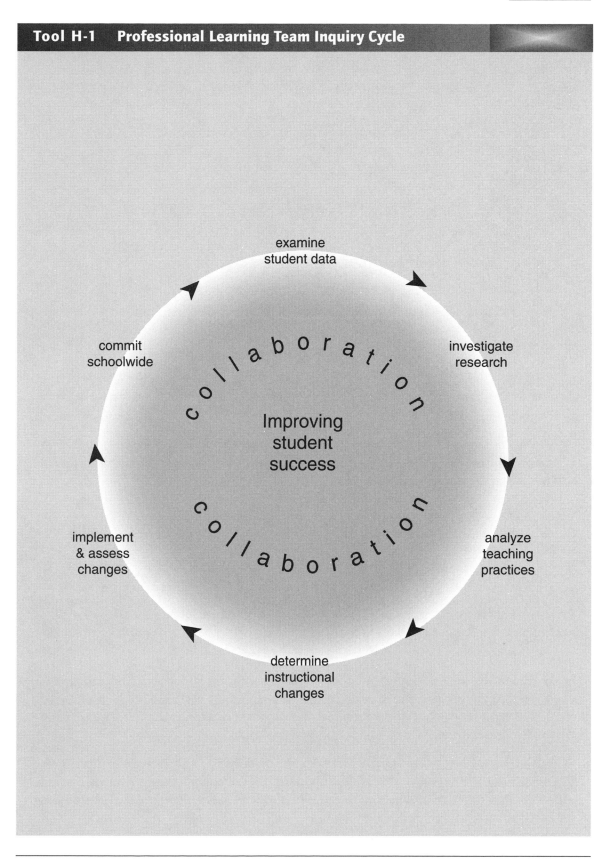

Tool H-2   PLT Inquiry Cycle With Steps Explained

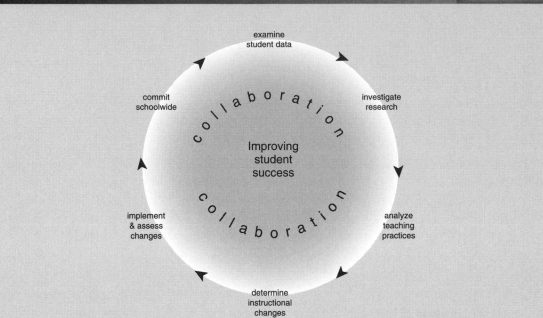

Examine Student Data—Teachers analyze a variety of student achievement and other data to identify specific learning challenges. These learning challenges become the focus for PLT inquiry.

Investigate Research—Teachers investigate research and best practices to identify evidence-based practices that will address the learning challenges.

Analyze Teaching Practices—Within their teams, teachers analyze their own practices as well as what's happening schoolwide to better understand how to improve learning for all students, not just the ones they serve.

Determine Instructional Changes—Based on their inquiry into data, research, and their own practices, teachers identify instructional changes to make.

Implement and Assess Changes—Teachers spend approximately two months trying out the new practices, deepening their knowledge and skills around classroom assessments, analyzing student work, observing each other, and tracking the performance of one or more focal point students' as a way to effectively improve teaching practices.

Commit Schoolwide—After determining which instructional changes resulted in improved student learning, each PLT presents the results of its inquiry to the school to adopt the proven instructional strategy schoolwide.

Tool H-3 Getting Started: Sample Agenda for Workshop 1

Goals for this session:

- Introduce the concept of Professional Learning Teams and the PLT Cycle of Inquiry
- Determine appropriate PLT topics through data analysis and data-driven decision making
- Facilitate the formation of PLTs based on specific guidelines and criteria
- Model strategies that support collaboration

Morning

Welcome and Introductions

- Review the goals, agenda, and logistics for the day
- Share expectations with each other

Journey Map—Looking back, considering the present, and looking forward

- Share successes, challenges, and lessons learned
- Envision the future
- Share experiences around teams and collaborative work

Introduction to Professional Learning Teams

- Explore the characteristics of Professional Learning Teams
- Introduce the PLT Inquiry Cycle

Lunch

Afternoon

Data Analysis and Identification of PLT Topics

- Participate in one of the main activities of a PLT: looking at data and making decisions based on that data

Formation of PLTs

- Forming PLTs based on the needs identified through the data analysis, following specific guidelines and criteria that balance schoolwide needs and goals with individual needs and goals

Next Steps, Evaluation

- Indentify next steps for the PLTs
- Introduce the PLC Survey
- Provide feedback to the trainer

Tool H-4   PLT Team Log Form

Date: _____   Time: _____ to _____   Location: _____

Team Members:

Present	Role	Absent

- Item 1: _____ Time Limit: _____

What was accomplished? What did we conclude and resolve to do next?

_____

_____

_____

_____

_____

- Item 2: _____ Time Limit: _____

What was accomplished? What did we conclude and resolve to do next?

_____

_____

_____

_____

_____

- Item 3: _____ Time Limit: _____

What was accomplished? What did we conclude and resolve to do next?

_____

_____

_____

_____

_____

Next Scheduled Meeting:

Date: _____   Time: _____   Location: _____

Facilitator: _____   Recorder: _____

Timekeeper: _____   Process Observer: _____

If your team has agreed to share your meeting notes, the recorder should copy and distribute this log before placing it in your team's notebook. Agreements and/or assignments can be recorded on the planning form.

Tool H-5 Sample PLT Team Meeting Agenda and Log

Date: 9/12/08   Time: 2:30 p.m.   to   3:30 p.m.   Location: Sarah's classroom

Team Members:

Present	Role	Absent
Gene	Facilitator	Lisa
Sarah	Time Keeper	
Alice	Recorder	
Jonathan	Process Observer	
Marie		

● **Agenda Item 1:** Develop our own Working Agreements—15 min.

Working Agreements:

(1) Begin and end on time.

(2) Silence cell phones.

(3) Encourage diverse opinions.

(4) Allow equal time—no one dominates.

We are adding a role: rotating responsibility for bringing a healthy snack to our meeting

● **Agenda Item 2:** Review findings from data on our specific students—25 min.

Data reveals our students learning challenges in reading and includes the following:

(1) Understanding and applying "Main Idea and Supporting Details"

(2) Discerning "Fact From Opinion"

(3) Interpreting meaning in nonfiction

(4) Making predictions

● **Agenda Item 3:** Select an area of focus for our inquiry (consensus)—10 min.

We will start with Main Idea and Supporting Details and look for specific strategies to help our students learn this skill. Next meeting, we will share what we have come up with in terms of strategies and decide how to measure mastery of this skill.

● **Process Observer report out:** We did a good job observing our agreements.

➔ **Agreements and/or Assignments are recorded on the Planning Form!**

Next Scheduled Meeting:

Date: 9/26/08   Time: 2:30   Location: Sarah's classroom

Facilitator: Marie   Recorder: Jonathan

Timekeeper: Gene   Process Observer: Sarah

Snacks: Alice

If your team has agreed to share your meeting notes, the Recorder should copy and distribute this log before placing it in your team's notebook.

Tool H-6   Defining Team Roles

At one time or another, all members of your Professional Learning Team (PLT) will fulfill the roles your PLT establishes. Having PLT members take responsibility for various critical team functions helps ensure that they are recognized and accomplished. In this way, individual members learn how to complete necessary tasks, and your PLT avoids becoming dominated by an individual with a stronger leadership background or tendencies. The PLT is also more likely to be effective when members assume these roles on a rotating basis each time the PLT convenes. Rotating roles ensures that all members have the opportunity to develop their leadership skills and exposes the PLT to different leadership styles.

Roles should remain flexible within the PLT. New roles may be created, and old ones retired as the needs of the team change. Initially, PLT roles might include the following:

Facilitator: Helps the team set the agenda, time, and place of the meeting and sends agenda out in advance and keeps discussions on topic

The Facilitator makes statements such as, "Let's stay on task" and asks, "Any more ideas?"

Recorder: Keeps track of the team's comments and decisions and through the written record, creates a group memory and facilitates sharing of information outside the team

The Recorder makes statements such as, "Let me make sure I wrote this down correctly" and asks, "What are our main points?"

Timekeeper: Makes sure each agenda item has an assigned length of time and keeps team apprised of how well it is moving through the agenda and suggests and manages any impromptu adjustments to the agenda

The Timekeeper makes statements such as, "We have five more minutes" and asks, "Should we discuss this topic now or wait until our next meeting?"

Process Observer: Reminds team of the ground rules and norms and notes when acceptable group procedures are and are not being followed.

The Process Observer makes statements such as, "Today we stayed on task" and "We didn't allow equal air time."

You may choose to add additional roles.

Tool H-7 Professional Learning Team: Planning Sheet

Tasks To Do	Why?	How?	Who?	By When?

Our Next Meeting is: _____ at _____ in room _____ Facilitator: _____
                    (date)   (time)   (location)   (name)

Tool H-8   Five Dimensions of Professional Learning Communities

Supportive and Shared Leadership

Shared Beliefs, Values, and Vision

Collective Learning
and
Application of That Learning

Supportive Conditions

Shared Personal Practice

Hord, Shirley M., & Sommers, William A. (2008, p.9)

Tool H-9   Criteria for Quality Team Time

Time should be **regular**:
the same day and time each week or biweekly

Time should be **job-embedded**:
within the normal contract day

Time should be **ongoing**:
a commitment for the entire school year
and beyond

Time should be of **sufficient duration** to promote
in-depth discussions and understanding:
at least an hour a week, or 90 minutes biweekly

Time should be **dedicated**
for professional learning only

Tool H-10   Finding Time for Collaboration

Eliminate

- Teacher duty periods to allow time for team-based professional development
- Traditional inservice days by redistributing time into shorter but more regular meetings
- Faculty meetings used for administrative duties that can be handled by e-mails, memos, or similar methods
- Activities that do not directly contribute to student achievement or staff professional learning; use those funds for substitutes or extended contract hours for PLTs

Use Extended Lunch

- In schools with a single, common lunch for all students, create time for staff team meetings by extending lunch once every week or every other week with parent volunteers or substitutes supervising students

Schedule Flex Time

- Allow teachers to arrive at school at different times, with adjustments to their departure times, to create a longer block either before or after school for team meetings

Hire Substitute Teachers or Administrative Substitutes

- Release teams of teachers during the workday for meetings, using a *regular team of substitutes to help ensure continuity in the classrooms*
- Use administrators as substitutes for some of the teachers, allowing them to get to know students in a different context and to showcase curricular and instructional strategies

Regularly Schedule Early Dismissal or Late Arrival for Students

- Lengthen some school days to allow more time on other days for team meetings
- Use time during some school days for students to engage in service learning or offer school-to-work internships to students

Establish Special Studies Day or Time

- Create a block or blocks of time throughout a week for all the students of one team of teachers to meet with specialists in the building, freeing that team to work together

Create a Four-Day Student Week

- Lengthen each school day to maintain student-teacher contact time and to enable staff to have one full day a week to meet in teams

Use Block and Modified-Block Schedules

- Create block schedules to provide longer periods of time for in-depth student and staff learning as teachers adopt instructional strategies suited to longer classes

Tool H-11   Factors Supporting the Success of PLTs

1. There is *collective participation and collaboration* that involves groups of teachers working together to solve problems and refine practice to improve learning for all students.

2. Professional learning is *content rich and student focused;* that is, teacher learning provides opportunities for teachers to develop strong expertise in the content areas they teach and in understanding how students learn that subject area.

3. Professional learning is *teacher led.* It is learning that addresses real problems teachers face in their classrooms and involves individual as well as collective reflection and inquiry into professional practice.

4. There is ample *time and duration* for professional learning. Professional learning must be sustained over time and involve a substantial number of contact hours.

5. Professional learning occurs in a *data-rich* environment where teachers use multiple sources of information to analyze student learning goals against student performance.

6. There is *strong, supportive, and shared leadership* for professional learning. The role of the principal is vital. Sharing leadership with teachers, developing collaborative decision-making processes, and cultivating opportunities and structures for teacher learning are examples of practices that support PLTs.

7. *External support* such as district-level or external facilitators is important for teachers to be exposed to fresh ideas, approaches, and perspectives that challenge traditional thinking.

8. PLTs are one component of a *coherent plan* for improving student success. Coherence means that professional learning is part of a larger school improvement effort and that it is planned over multiple years, focused on specific goals tied to student learning.

Tool H-12   PLT Implementation Rubric

Developed by Jacqueline Raphael, Northwest Regional Educational Laboratory

PLT Name: _____

School: _____

Directions: For each page, please place an X on the most accurate rating (level 1, 2, 3, 4, or 5) corresponding to each feature listed in the horizontal rows.

Place the X over the text if marking levels 1, 3, or 5 and in the blank box if marking levels 2 or 4.

Thank you.

(I) Our PLT is well supported by the school organization and leadership.

Components	Level 1	Level 2	Level 3	Level 4	Level 5
Dedicating sufficient time for PLTs	Our school dedicates little or no time to PLTs.		Our school dedicates some time (e.g., 60 minutes every other week) to PLTs, but that time is not part of the regular daily schedule and is sometimes used for other purposes.		Our school dedicates sufficient time (e.g., 60 to 90 minutes every other week or weekly) to PLTs as part of the regular daily schedule.
Ensuring accountability to school administrators and each other	Our PLT does not document that our time is used efficiently and is focused on PLT goals (e.g., changing instruction to improve student learning)		Our PLT documents that our time is used efficiently, typically with logs, although we do not have to show progress and there are no major consequences if we do not establish or achieve goals.		Our PLT documents that our time is used efficiently, that our work remains focused, and that we achieve the goals we have set, using logs, action plans, and other tools. There are consequences if we do not document these outcomes.
Allowing teachers to direct efforts	Our PLT work is defined by the goals and approaches of school or district administrators.		Our PLT work is somewhat led by our teachers, in that we define some of our goals, but school or district administrators limit the topics or approaches we can investigate; our work often fits into their requirements.		Our PLT work is led by our teachers, who are encouraged to define our goals based on data and to identify our focus as well as the specific topics, strategies, and approaches we investigate.
Encouraging instructional change	Our school leaders rarely address how teachers change instruction.		Our school leaders sometimes encourage teachers to change instruction, but often in general terms and without giving specific constructive feedback.		Our school leaders regularly encourage teachers to change instruction after observing frequently and providing specific suggestions.
Sharing leadership for decision making	The majority of our school decisions are made autocratically by the principal.		Many of our school decisions are made through collaborative processes involving teachers, but some of the most important decisions are still made primarily by administrators, perhaps with a select few teachers.		Most of our school decisions are based on research and data and are made with all staff willingly participating in collaborative decision-making; consensus is used appropriately.

(2) Our PLT uses student achievement and other types of data to promote student learning.

Components	Level 1	Level 2	Level 3	Level 4	Level 5
Establishing a PLT topic	Our PLT uses little or no student data (e.g., achievement data, classroom data) to establish our PLT focus.		Our PLT uses a limited variety of data (e.g., percent of students meeting standards) to establish our PLT focus.		Our PLT uses a wide variety of data, including student achievement and classroom data, to establish our PLT focus.
Using data to make decisions related to improving student learning	Our PLT uses no data to make decisions and set goals.		Our PLT occasionally uses student achievement and classroom data to make decisions and set goals, although these data are usually school or classroom averages (i.e., not disaggregated).		Our PLT routinely uses student achievement and classroom data disaggregated by individual student and student subgroups, as well as content areas, and over time where possible.
Assessing current classroom (e.g., curricular, instructional, and assessment-related) practices	Our PLT collects little or no data to assess current classroom practice.		Our PLT collects some data on classroom practices, but data tend to be incomplete and are not collected from all teachers.		Our PLT collects classroom practice data systematically (e.g., through surveys, observation checklists, etc.) from all teachers on specified practices.
Monitoring teacher efforts to adapt classroom practices to improve student learning	Our PLT collects little or no data (e.g., classroom assessment results) to determine effects of new/refined practices on student learning.		Our PLT collects some data to determine effects of new practices on student learning, but the data or analyses tend to be incomplete.		Our PLT collects and analyzes sufficient data to reasonably conclude whether the new practices appear likely to positively affect student learning.

(3) Our PLT shares and reflects on classroom practice.

Components	Level 1	Level 2	Level 3	Level 4	Level 5
Reflecting individually on classroom practices to promote student learning	Individual teachers in our PLT rarely reflect on their classroom practices.		Teachers in our PLT sometimes reflect on their classroom practices but usually not deeply.		Teachers in our PLT regularly reflect on their classroom practices through the use of tools and activities that lead to deep-level reflection.
Sharing and reflecting on classroom practices with PLT members to promote student learning	Our PLT rarely shares and reflects on classroom practices together.		Our PLT sometimes shares and reflects on classroom practices together but often in informal discussions (e.g., "hallway talk") between one or two teachers and only sometimes using structured methods to promote greater understanding.		Our PLT regularly shares and reflects on classroom practices together using structured methods (e.g., analyzing student work) that promote continuous improvement and deep reflection on teacher beliefs.
Sharing experiences and student outcomes when first using new or improved classroom practices to promote student learning	Our PLT rarely shares its experiences and student outcomes when using new or improved classroom practices.		Our PLT sometimes shares its experiences and student outcomes when using new or improved classroom practices, but often in informal discussions between one or two teachers and not systematically, as part of their PLT work.		Our PLT members regularly share their experiences and student outcomes related to new or improved classroom practices using structured methods (e.g., analyzing student work) and data collection plans.
Observing in other teachers' classrooms	Teachers in our PLT rarely observe in other teachers' classrooms.		Teachers in our PLT sometimes observe in other teachers' classrooms, usually without meeting in advance to establish common understanding of the lesson or after to debrief and reflect on the lesson.		Teachers in our PLT often observe in other teachers' classrooms, meeting in advance to review lesson goals and purpose of the observation, and afterward to debrief and reflect on the lesson.

(4) Our PLT studies and uses research to improve student learning.

Components	Level 1	Level 2	Level 3	Level 4	Level 5
Reading research and best practices related to PLT topic	Our PLT rarely reads professional journals and research related to our PLT topic.		Our PLT reads professional journals and research related to our PLT topic when asked to.		Our PLT regularly reads professional journals and research related to our PLT topic and shares findings with the team.
Analyzing and evaluating research and best practices related to PLT topic	Our PLT rarely analyzes and evaluates research and best practices related to our PLT topic.		Our PLT sometimes analyzes and evaluates research and best practices related to our PLT topic but mainly when this is required and only occasionally using structured methods that promote deep analysis.		Our PLT regularly analyzes and evaluates research and best practices related to our PLT topic, using tools that promote deep analysis.
Analyzing a variety of research and best practices related to PLT topic	Our PLT does not analyze a variety of research and best practices related our PLT topic.		Our PLT analyzes informed opinions on best practices and possibly a piece of qualitative or quantitative research related to our PLT topic.		Our PLT regularly analyzes a variety of informed opinions on best practices, as well as qualitative and quantitative research related to our PLT topic. When possible, we review the research cited by the authors of opinion pieces. We include any seminal research related to our PLT topic in discussions.
Using research and best practices to identify new practices to implement (or current practices to refine)	Our PLT rarely identifies new classroom practices to implement (or current practices to refine) based on research and best practices.		Our PLT sometimes identifies new classroom practices to implement (or current practices to refine) based on research and best practices, often without reading sufficiently about the contexts (i.e., students and school) in which these practices have been successful.		Our PLT regularly identifies new classroom practices to implement (or current practices to refine) based on research and best practices with a deep understanding of the contexts in which these practices have been successful.

(5) Our PLT increases its use of research-based classroom practices.

Components	Level 1	Level 2	Level 3	Level 4	Level 5
Using appropriate research-based practices	Our PLT rarely changes classroom practices based on research and best practices.		Our PLT sometimes changes classroom practices, based on research and best practices but without complete understanding of the contexts in which these practices have been successful.		Our PLT changes classroom practices based on research and best practices with a rich understanding of the contexts in which these practices have been successful.
Improving the quality of classroom practices	Our PLT rarely changes classroom practices with a clear picture of what effective use of the practice looks like.		Our PLT changes classroom practices, often without a clear picture of what effective use of the practice looks like.		Our PLT changes classroom practices based on a clear picture of how to use the practice in our classrooms through activities such as completing an implementation matrix and observing at other schools.
Giving changes in classroom practice sufficient time to work	Our PLT rarely changes classroom practice for more than a brief period of time.		Our PLT changes classroom practices but not over a sufficient period of time (i.e., at least two months) and only sometimes sharing our progress with our PLT.		Our PLT changes classroom practices consistently over at least two months, keeping records we regularly share with our PLT.
Drawing conclusions about strategies and practices	Our PLT rarely draws conclusions about changing classroom practices.		Our PLT draws conclusions about changing classroom practices, but these are not often based on data we collected and do not always represent a consensus view.		Our PLT draws conclusions about changing classroom practice after following a well-documented plan leading to a consensus about next steps around new practices.

(6) Our PLT uses effective collaborative and teamwork skills.

Components	Level 1	Level 2	Level 3	Level 4	Level 5
Using effective team strategies to enhance productivity of PLT efforts	Our PLT rarely uses effective team strategies (e.g., clearly defined team roles, agendas, logs, norms).		Our PLT uses some effective team strategies (e.g, clearly defined team roles, agendas, logs, norms) but not consistently and not always successfully.		Our PLT consistently and successfully uses effective team strategies.
Addressing conflict productively to deepen understanding of differences	Our PLT usually avoids conflict through the use of inappropriate strategies.		Our PLT is beginning to address conflict in appropriate ways.		Our PLT resolves conflict in appropriate ways and to everyone's satisfaction using a collaboratively designed plan.
Communicating clearly and consistently	Our PLT communication is unclear and inconsistent.		Our PLT communication is improving but misunderstandings continue to arise.		Our PLT communication is clear and consistent.
Collaborating on activities	Teachers in our PLT work in isolation.		Some teachers in our PLT collaborate while others work in isolation.		Our PLT collaborates regularly.
Reflecting on team dynamics	Our PLT spends little time reflecting on team dynamics (i.e., how well they are working, learning, and improving practices together).		Our PLT spends some time reflecting on team dynamics but not consistently and without keeping a record of progress.		Our PLT regularly reflects on team dynamics (i.e., how well we are working, learning, and improving practices together) in ways that ensure feedback from all and a record of progress.
Building and maintaining trust	Our PLT lacks trust among individual members, which limits our ability to work together.		Our PLT is making progress in building trust among members, but we still have a way to go.		Our PLT has a high level of trust that contributes to our productivity and ability to work through issues when they come up.
Celebrating successes of PLT to reinforce strengths and lessons learned	Our PLT does not celebrate successes.		Our PLT acknowledges successes but does not usually acknowledge the individuals who made the efforts, measure the gains that have been made, or reflect on lessons learned.		Our PLT regularly reinforces successes by acknowledging individual and group efforts, and by measuring gains and reflecting on lessons learned.

Tool H-13   Getting Started Roadmap

This resource provides an abbreviated guide to assist schools in getting started developing PLTs. For more in-depth information and the research underlying PLTs, refer to the main chapters in this book. In particular, refer to the Action items identified throughout the text by the *Action Icon* as well as the *Leadership Team Discussion* section at the end of each chapter. The following brief roadmap provides a quick view of important issues to consider in getting started, while subsequent pages contain a chapter by chapter summary.

Getting Started Roadmap in Brief

Beginning:

- Develop an understanding of Professional Learning Teams.
- Start planning several months ahead of time.
- Assemble a leadership team that includes some teachers.

Foundational Issues:

- Assess the school's readiness for change.
- Decide whether you need an outside facilitator to train the staff in the PLT process. If not, who in the school or district is best qualified to conduct training?

Relational Issues:

- Assess the current trust level in your school and plan ways to increase it; include relationship building in your roll out plans.
- Make sure you have adequate avenues for communicating with all constituents; if not, develop some new ways to get the word out.
- Prepare for conflict ahead of time.

Practical Issues:

- Keep staff in the information loop.
- Advocate for PLTs with all constituents:
  o District office
  o School board
  o Teachers' union
  o Parents
  o Community members

- Assure provision of adequate time for PLT training and team meetings.
- Prepare to provide current data to teachers along with training to understand and interpret data.
- Provide additional resources to support the success of your PLTs.
- Establish a system of supportive accountability.
- Plan to use the PLT rubric to encourage teachers' reflection and self-monitoring.
- Anticipate and prepare for some of the potential challenges.

Leadership

- Understand and build shared and facilitative leadership.
- Develop a strong foundation in instructional leadership.
- Plan for administrators to have a visible profile throughout the school.
- Support the growth of teacher leadership.
- Plan for leadership sustainability.
- Reinforce PLT strategies and skills in other meetings.
- Assure that PLTs are teacher led.

(Continued)

(Continued)

Chapter 1: Understanding Professional Learning Teams

Professional learning teams (PLTs) are groups of four to six teachers from the same school, department, or grade level who come together to help each other improve student learning by changing classroom instruction. PLTs are goal oriented and maintain an unrelenting focus on student learning. In PLTs, teachers work in small, self-selected teams to do the following:

- Examine disaggregated student achievement and classroom data and use these findings as a basis for making decisions and choosing instructional practices to focus improvement efforts
- Select a specific area of student need to investigate as a focus for strengthening or changing practice
- Frame an inquiry question to guide the PLT's work
- Use educational research to build their knowledge base and inform decisions in choosing new strategies and best practices for teaching their students
- Analyze current teaching practices throughout the school to identify successful practices already in place as well as to understand schoolwide needs
- Implement decisions by trying out new teaching practices or honing existing successful practices
- Collect classroom data to document activities and assess the effects of new strategies
- Work collaboratively and share their practice and expertise through reflective dialogue, analysis of student work, and observing each other's classroom practices
- Function effectively as a team by paying attention to collaboration and documenting team activities
- Sharing the focus and results of each team's work with the greater schoolwide community

Teachers in PLTs work together by doing the following:

- Meeting on a regular basis to support and learn from each other
- Sharing classroom practices with their colleagues
- Committing to improve their practice and support their colleagues in doing the same
- Seeking to improve their collaboration skills and apply them to effective PLTs and to the classroom

PLTs work within their own content areas as well as school and district curriculum guidelines with a focus on improving student learning and achievement. Ideally, the school staff is organized into small groups—PLTs—of four to six people, who get to know and trust one another. Teams are kept small enough so they can accomplish the work yet large enough to have divergent opinions that stimulate discussion. Teams may be organized by grade level, content area, or specific interests that emerge from examining data. Interdisciplinary teams offer the opportunity for teachers to learn about different content areas and their specific ways of teaching. When teams collaborate to implement the same strategies in multiple content areas, students can benefit as they move from class to class or different grade levels and bring an understanding of the process with them. The decision to form interdisciplinary teams or organize around some other appropriate factor, such as a department or common goal, should be made thoughtfully. Some schools also include vertical curriculum teams who meet less often, but work together to assure articulation of goals and curricula from grade to grade in the entire school. Members may switch teams based on shifting student needs and teachers' own interests and expertise.

PLTs follow the inquiry cycle illustrated below. This cycle can take a full year and sometimes more to complete for the first time.

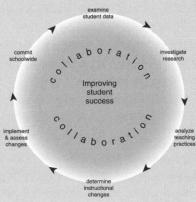

It should be noted that PLTs are distinct from school committees. A PLT comes together at least biweekly to meet with a direct focus on improving students' learning and academic success. This usually involves instituting changes in classroom instruction. A committee, on the other hand, is a temporary group formed to focus on specific needs within the school other than student learning; a committee may deal with issues such as student rules (dress code, attendance policy, and discipline issues), school climate, parent engagement, and so on. Committees focusing on a specific predetermined set of topics have as much importance as PLTs. The main difference is that a committee may disband once it has accomplished its purpose. PLTs, on the other hand, will provide a greater benefit to the school if they are ongoing and embedded in the way teachers collaborate to focus on student learning and instruction.

See Chapter 1 for in-depth information on PLTs, including the following:

- The research support for the process:
  - The need for PLTs
  - Teacher quality as a critical factor in improving learning
  - Teachers' need for more than classroom experience to be effective
  - The limitations of traditional professional development
  - Team-based learning (collaboration) does improve practice

- A sample timeline for the first year of PLT implementation (Table 1)
- Features of effective professional development (Table 2) that inform the PLT process
- A description of some other models for teacher collaboration; these are compatible with or may be adapted for use with the PLT model, especially Action Research, Lesson Study, Data Teams, and Looking at Student Work.

The questions to guide early leadership team discussions, found at the end of each chapter, can help guide discussion early in the planning process.

Chapter 2: Setting the Stage for Success

Readiness for Change. To assure a higher level of success in implementing the PLT process, school leaders will benefit by allocating sufficient planning time to lay the groundwork within the school, the district, and the community, including parents. There are many tools for assessing a school's readiness for change; two of these online surveys are described in Resource B and Resource C. These tools cannot only indicate potential areas needing extra attention, but they also can provide a way to measure ongoing success of change efforts. Instituting a collaborative work process into the school may be a radical change for the staff. The PLT process itself, which asks teachers to share their practice openly with colleagues, can be threatening to some individuals accustomed to closing their door and teaching in isolation. Teachers as well as school leaders will benefit by developing a clear understanding of proposed changes. Everyone will appreciate information about the proposed change; how it will affect each individual administrator, teacher, and student; and some reassurance that they will receive support during the process.

Trust. Intentional efforts to build and maintain trust, develop ways to work with conflict, and create or strengthen avenues of communication are crucial to the success of PLTs as a job embedded form of professional development. Building and nurturing trust in schools is essential if teachers are to work collaboratively. The entire school will reap the benefit when relationships are nurtured with an eye to creating a safe environment where teachers feel free to share both success and challenges with colleagues as they implement new teaching strategies. School leaders are encouraged to initiate, model, and continually nurture trusting relationships among staff. It is essential to make it safe for teachers to try something new, to take a risk, to experiment with sometimes daring strategies, and occasionally to realize the strategies didn't work as envisioned. Thus, it becomes safe to admit a mistake, to learn from that experience, and to regroup and try something else. This requires leaders to work at trust building with staff as well as to communicate a sense of confidence in teachers: a belief that they can change their practice in ways that result in enhanced learning and achievement for their students. This parallels the need for teachers to express their belief in their students' abilities to change and learn increasingly complex concepts—to achieve at higher and higher levels.

Building Relationships. At the heart of creating a safe environment is relationship building. Working and learning together in teams is a complex process that requires individuals to understand themselves, their beliefs, thoughts, and motives. Part of the groundwork for building relationships takes place when teams develop *norms* or a set of working agreements. These agreements should be revisited and revised from time to time to ensure they fit for the team members'

(Continued)

(Continued)

needs. Teams may change some members from year to year. It is important to revise working agreements to support the new team, assuring that each teacher has a voice.

Working With Conflict. PLTs are intentionally kept small with only four to six members in a team. The limited size ensures that everyone participates fully in the process. It also provides enough individual voices to encourage diverse opinions and thoughts. Keeping teams small has the added benefit of making it easier to resolve the inevitable conflicts and disagreements. Some level of conflict is inevitable in any group, particularly one with an emphasis on changing the status quo. Healthy organizations use conflict as an opportunity to grow while exploring divergent points of view.

What schools do to prepare for conflict is an important aspect of supporting PLTs. For many people conflict can be disconcerting, something to be avoided. This can drive problems underground and undermine the team's cohesion and work. Acknowledging and working with conflict can help promote individual and organizational learning and growth. Debate and controversy can be positive elements in a school's culture when individuals consciously work to maintain a constructive level of conflict and debate while keeping a respectful attitude. Conflict offers a context for inquiry, organizational learning, and change. As colleagues air differences, build understanding across perspectives, and see changes enhanced by divergent thinking, conflict becomes constructive for the school community.

Viewing conflict as an opportunity for growth, a chance to explore differences and learn from and about each other, can dispel fear and guard against avoidance. In this way, conflict can be reframed as positive and play an important part in the development of healthy work relationships. Rather than trying to head off conflict at every turn, it is important to acknowledge the potential and use the opportunity to learn and grow together. See Resource E for one model for resolving conflict. There are other models and schools are encouraged to select and practice with their model early on so it becomes a useful and ready tool. Resource F contains some sample conflict scenarios for teams to practice resolving conflicts prior to working with their own real conflicts in the school.

Creating Avenues of Communication. The PLT planning process provides an opportune time to think about how communication occurs within the school; between the school, parents, and community; with other schools; and with the district office. It is highly important to share information about change efforts up front with others in the school community in order to develop buy-in and anticipate some of the challenges that may occur during implementation. The most effective communication is often face-to-face rather than by e-mail or newsletters. Information needs to be shared with the entire school community, especially the district office and school board. It can be especially important to involve the teachers' union and elicit their support along with parents and the community.

Teachers will be responsible for implementing PLTs. They are closest to the action in classrooms and the primary movers in the change process in any school. Teacher representatives should be included on the planning committee and leadership team. Their understanding and buy-in to the process are essential for success. Thus, they must be kept respectfully in the information loop during the planning process. It is important to provide regular updates to the entire staff so there are no surprises. Teacher leaders themselves may be the best emissaries to keep staff informed. We recommend involving the entire staff in making important decisions that affect their work and lives.

An ancillary step in communication is to listen to the naysayers to understand their point of view and possibly circumvent potential problems. On every teaching staff you will likely find three types of participants: some teachers will enthusiastically embrace change efforts; some will adopt a *wait-and-see* stance; and a few will openly or covertly resist the change. Those resisters may have important information to consider during both planning and implementation. When possible, an effective method of involving and informing some of the resisters is to send them to visit a school that is successfully implementing the PLT process. (For additional suggestions on dealing with the resisters, see Chapter 5.)

The classified staff is sometimes more closely connected to the community than teachers are and to parents in particular. They need to be kept informed about proposed changes, particularly since scheduling changes may affect their workday. In addition, they may need to respond to informal questions from parents and community members. In some schools, paraprofessionals more directly reflect the community. They may be the only staff members who speak the same language as some of the parents. Another early decision to be discussed in planning PLTs is whether teams will include paraprofessionals.

Chapter 3: Laying the Foundation Within the School Community

Advocating for PLTs With Important Stakeholders. In order to keep all stakeholders informed during the planning phase, develop regular ways to communicate with people outside the school. You may need to advocate for changes in the school schedule or additional time for teachers to meet. First of all, communicate regularly with key individuals in the district office and plan ways to inform the school board; their support can be crucial to the success of your efforts. Some of the research found within the chapters of this book may be used to provide a rationale for PLTs and some of the other tools in this section may be useful. Remember to elicit support from the teacher's union and parents who may be affected by schedule changes. Information to parents can include a simplified rationale and expected outcomes.

Aligning With School Goals. All professional development benefits when it is a coherent part of the long-term plan for school improvement and aligns with school and district goals. Teachers need to understand the school improvement plan in order to coordinate their teamwork with these goals. If more pressing needs have come up since the plan was written, it may be time for revision.

Structures for Working Collaboratively. Two of the structures that support collaboration are the leadership team and allocating sufficient time for teachers to work in their PLTs. The leadership team can be a valuable way to model collaboration, shared decision making, and elicit teacher buy-in. The composition of this team matters. If some members are teacher leaders who command respect from colleagues, they can be valuable allies in eliciting staff support.

To be successful, teachers need regularly scheduled time to meet together in their teams to accomplish their agreed upon work. Ideally, they meet for at least 90 minutes twice a month or 60 minutes weekly. It is important that this time is protected to ensure that PLT members have the time to be successful in changing their practices. If PLT time is frequently co-opted for other uses, the work of the teams will be diluted in ways that diminish outcomes. Meeting more frequently is desirable—limiting time to one long monthly meeting interrupts the flow of team thinking and may make it challenging for teachers to focus on group efforts to improve student learning. Quality team time requires a commitment by both administrators and teachers. See Resource D for examples of how other schools have allocated time for teacher professional development. **Tool H-9** *Criteria for Quality Team Time* sets out important conditions for time. **Tool H-10** *Finding Time for Collaboration* summarizes suggested ways to identify time while Resource D provides examples of the ways some schools have carved out time for teachers to collaborate.

Providing and Using Data. PLTs use data at three important times in the process. First, they use schoolwide achievement data to begin to pinpoint student learning needs. They may establish teams based on teacher self-selection according to teachers' interests and desire to tackle specific areas. Next, each team digs deeper into the data on their own students, using its findings to develop a focus question to guide their efforts. Finally, teams develop ways to assess student learning related to their specific focus and use that data to monitor ongoing progress. While the annual test data serve as a starting point, teams are encouraged to use more specific measures, develop common assessments and other ways to measure incremental progress, and make adjustments to teaching strategies when appropriate.

The challenge for leaders is to provide data in user-friendly formats along with sufficient training for teachers to access and interpret data. Standardized test results disaggregated by grade level, ethnicity, gender, economic status, and language ability will be more useful if those scores can be broken down to provide strand information with more detail about the skills students may be missing in academic content areas. Attendance patterns, disciplinary referrals, course enrollment and completion, grading patterns, dropout statistics, and school climate measures help round out the picture of school and student challenges. Teams can then examine data to better understand their own students' needs and pinpoint the focus for their inquiry. Teachers benefit when they set their own goals and monitor student progress toward meeting those goals.

Providing Additional Resources. Teachers will need some additional resources as they proceed with their PLTs. Providing resources up front will ease the way and help them feel like professionals. Some of those resources may include the following:

- Space—a comfortable, quiet place for team meetings
- Accessible storage—a file cabinet for storing common materials such as research articles and information on new teaching strategies
- Materials—notebooks to store team materials—working agreements, meeting logs, training materials, student data, research, and details about teaching strategies. See tools **H-4** and **H-5** for a suggested format and example of a team meeting agenda and log; this tool is purposefully kept brief so as not to add a burdensome level of record keeping.
- Tools **H-6** *Defining Team Roles* and **H-7** *Planning Sheet* can be distributed to teams to assist them in understanding and using team roles and planning their work at the end of each meeting.
- Professional library—this may include professional books and subscriptions to useful journals
- Research—providing some research up-front may spur teachers to do additional searching either online or in the library. In many schools the librarian can assist in the search for related research.
- External support—this can be facilitation and training for staff during the startup phase, as well as training in specific content areas.

(Continued)

(Continued)

Establishing Supportive Accountability. Staff members need to be accountable for effective use of their team time. It may elicit more teacher buy-in when teachers are collaboratively engaged in the development, refinement, and reporting for accountability. When using Tool **H-4** *PLT Team Log Form,* teams do need to record their decisions and reasons for making those choices as well as subsequent actions. This will assist them as they reflect back on the success and challenges of their efforts—the process they used and their accomplishments. Keeping a team notebook documents activities and maintains a rich record of the work. If school leaders have access to these notebooks, with teachers' consent, it adds a level of transparency and accountability for each team. Teams may choose to make their logs public, either online or posted in a common place, to contribute to the larger Professional Learning Community within the school.

Scheduling regular times for schoolwide sharing of each team's work can provide public accountability as well as allow groups to benefit through understanding the work of their colleagues. This helps reinforce a shared vision for school improvement focused on effective teaching and learning. It keeps teams connected to each other and the larger school community. Early on, teams may share their findings from examination of data and the direction they are choosing for inquiry. At midyear they may share progress including the research they are using. Combined with the results of an analysis on schoolwide teaching practices, this information can stimulate thinking among all teams. Near the end of the school year, teams are asked to make more formal presentations that include the focus question, related research, chosen strategies, common assessment, and results. For successful strategies, the team may make a case for other PLTs or even the entire school to adopt successful strategies. However, it is still important to hear from teams who may have had less success. Speculation about the results of their work is important. Remember, it needs to be safe to share this kind of information as well as the sparkling results of other teams. There can be important lessons to learn from the efforts of all teams.

Chapter 4: What About Leadership?

Administrators as Instructional Leaders. The understanding and support of school and district administrators is a crucial element in school change. They signify their support in multiple ways—attending PLT training and applying some of the strategies in their own capacity. They can be significant role models for teachers as they continue to share their own learning with staff. In addition, it has been shown that there is a definite connection between school leadership and student achievement (see Chapter 4). Perhaps most important is the notion of developing instructional leadership capacity. Administrators as learners question, investigate, and seek solutions for challenges in school improvement and student achievement. Leaders, while not expected to be experts in all content areas, can learn to recognize quality teaching and effective instruction resulting in student engagement and learning. They can develop and support a culture of inquiry within the school. In conducting ongoing dialogue around school change, they introduce teachers to new research and strategies from their own reading and training. They can frame their own focusing questions and guide the leadership team in following the PLT inquiry cycle. They model ongoing learning while thoughtfully leading the school through change. Onsite coaching for school leaders can assist them in developing their own leadership skills.

Being Visible Throughout the School. Establishing relationships with staff that allows administrators to enter classrooms at any time (nonevaluative) helps with visibility. Leaders can then experience teaching and learning as it happens, providing insights into how PLTs play out with students. Developing the walk-through process is one productive way to do this while strengthening instructional leadership knowledge and skills. The walk-through can influence real change in schools by getting administrators close to the classroom. It is purposefully kept separate from teacher evaluation. The walk-through is usually conducted by the principal and an assistant principal or supervising administrator. This provides an opportunity to observe curriculum and teaching in action. After each visit, administrators can discuss their perceptions with each other to deepen their own understanding of classroom teaching and learning. When the walk-through is well implemented and kept separate from evaluation, teachers appreciate input from their administrators. Administrators may also attend some PLT meetings to understand the team's work. However, the PLT itself needs to be teacher led.

Shared and Facilitative Leadership. Principals have the power to affect student learning by setting a clear direction for change, focusing on success, and supporting staff learning. Effective professional learning communities depend on an open and facilitative leadership style that demonstrates in tangible terms that every adult in the school—like every student—must engage in a learning process. Teachers, as well as students, benefit when they take ownership of their own learning. This evolves into taking ownership of the authority needed to create a better learning environment for students.

Teacher Leadership. Shared leadership requires administrator understanding, encouragement, and support for others as they assume leadership roles. This also means recognizing when others are ready to assume more leadership responsibility. Principals need to be willing to develop and sustain conditions that support others to exercise leadership. Some of the more successful principals work collaboratively with teacher leaders with respect for the teaching culture. Teacher leaders can make a difference in schools. Working in teams focused on improving instruction, rotating roles and responsibilities, dealing with conflict when it arises, all support teachers in developing their own leadership skills. This depends on the administrator's ability to allow PLTs to be teacher led while maintaining supportive understanding of what goes on in those teams. The principal may need to step back and let teachers lead by owning the process. When a team may pursue a line of inquiry that she disagrees with, it honors teachers' professionalism to allow the team to learn their own lessons. This does not mean abandoning teachers or teams. It behooves school administrators to remain involved with the PLTs and to be aware of the direction each team takes: their focus questions, suggested strategies, implementation efforts, methods of assessment, challenges and successes. Knowledge about each PLT opens the door for administrators to provide their support and guidance.

Sustaining Leadership. Thought and planning for leadership succession and sustainability pays off. Sought-after changes and improvements within the school should not be contingent on a single, charismatic leader. Instead, leadership can be developed among many individuals in order to represent shared values and vision for change. When leadership is shared, the most valuable aspects of change can be advanced from one leader to the next. This doesn't happen automatically—it requires intentional planning, ongoing dialogue, and congruent actions by administrators. See Chapter 4 for suggestions from research on sustaining leadership.

A Professional Learning Team in Action. This vignette included at the end of Chapter 4 describes the process that one school employed to institute PLTs. Other schools choose different routes to developing PLTs.

Chapter 5: Supporting the Work of PLTs

Supporting Success. Eight factors, identified in the research literature, support the success of PLTs. These are addressed throughout the publication and summarized here and in Tool H-11 to highlight their importance. These factors are interdependent and equally significant; attending to each factor in planning and startup activities will pave the way for success.

1. There is *collective participation and collaboration* that involves groups of teachers working together to solve problems and refine practice to improve learning for all students.
2. Professional learning is *content rich and student focused*; that is, teacher learning provides opportunities for teachers to develop strong expertise in the content areas they teach and in understanding how students learn that subject area.
3. Professional learning is *teacher led*; it is learning that addresses real problems teachers face in their classrooms and involves individual as well as collective reflection and inquiry into professional practice.
4. There is *ample time and duration* for professional learning; staff learning must be sustained over time and involve a substantial number of contact hours.
5. Professional learning occurs in a *data-rich* environment where teachers use multiple sources of information to analyze student-learning goals against student performance.
6. There is *strong, supportive, and shared leadership* for professional learning. The role of the principal is vital. Sharing instructional leadership with teachers, developing collaborative decision-making processes, and cultivating opportunities and structures for teacher learning are examples of practices that support PLTs.
7. *External support* such as district-level or external facilitators is important for teachers to be exposed to fresh ideas, approaches, and perspectives that challenge traditional thinking.
8. PLTs are one component of a *coherent plan* for improving student success. Coherence means that professional learning is part of a larger school improvement effort that it is planned over multiple years and focused on specific goals tied to student learning.

Reinforcing PLT Strategies and Skills. Leaders make a powerful statement about the value of collaboration when they attend all training and use PLT strategies in other meetings. For instance, using an agenda with time limits for each item, keeping meeting minutes, posting minutes in a public place, and using and rotating defined team roles all reinforce collaboration skills. The school may benefit from a jointly developed set of schoolwide working agreements that are posted and reinforced. Reflecting on how well they follow these working agreements helps everyone become a productive member of the school community. The entire staff can share responsibility for monitoring norms and speaking up when they feel the agreements are not being followed. All of these strategies lead to more effective and collaborative meetings, and teachers may also use them in classrooms with students.

Leaders develop the capacity of their staff when they model and reinforce the value of continuous learning and research use by sharing key concepts from their own reading, distributing pertinent articles, and providing time at staff meetings to discuss these articles or other research. It is helpful to provide teachers with some of the current research supporting the focus of each PLT. Leaders can support teachers in pursuing other professional development opportunities and provide ways for those teachers to share their learning with the rest of the staff. Some schools have turned staff meeting time into professional development, including PLT training and meetings.

(Continued)

(Continued)

Ensuring That PLTs Are Teacher Led. Leaders benefit when they accurately assess the need to step in with some leadership as well as when it is time to back off and allow teachers to lead. It is important not to abandon teams while also resisting the urge to take over and lead a floundering team. Instead, help team members develop their own leadership skills. Assuring sufficient teacher representation on the leadership team can help leaders stay in touch with teachers. However, leaders also need to connect with individual teams to understand their work and provide essential support. Give some thought in planning about how teams will be formed. Will they be grade level, content area, or interdisciplinary? Allowing some teacher voice in team composition may result in a higher level of participation and implementation. One way to do this, after examining data and identifying specific student learning needs, is to allow teachers to choose a team based on their own interests, expertise, and desire to learn more about curriculum and instruction in an area of student need. When teachers develop their own focusing question(s) to guide their inquiry, they usually develop a related sense of commitment to the team.

Remember, learning to work collaboratively while examining and sharing their own classroom practice may be challenging for some teachers. While there are natural collaborators on any staff, there may be others who resist the process. One principal suggests, "[C]reate conditions that empower teachers." Listen more and let teachers do the talking. Facilitate but don't dominate meetings. This does not translate to abandonment. Let the process be teacher driven while providing resources and support, even modeling facilitative leadership when needed.

Using a Rubric to Encourage Reflection. See Tool **H-12** for a copy of the *PLT Implementation Rubric*. This rubric should not be used to evaluate teachers or teams; it is intended to assist teachers in reflecting and assessing their own progress as a team. This can be a valuable tool when a team takes one dimension at a time; each member rates their sense of where the team is on each component of that dimension. For instance, each team member receives a copy of that dimension, marks an *X* individually where they think their team is on each component; then the whole team compares ratings and discusses what is working and where they might want to improve. Allowing teams to use the rubric in this way supports their autonomy as well as the PLT process itself. It may be important for each team to develop their own set of *safe strategies* or conditions they need to engage in open discussion of team strengths and needs.

Anticipating Potential Challenges. See the section in Chapter 5 for a discussion of some of the challenges that have come up during PLT implementation in schools. These are by no means all possible challenges but a sampling with some suggested ideas for addressing them. Some of these challenges include the following:

- Finding time for training and meetings
- Dealing with the naysayers and those who do not attend training or participate in PLTs
- Working with changes in school leadership
- What about team leaders who do not believe in the process
- Getting teachers to locate their own research
- Resentment of an outside facilitator
- Countering the perception of PLT as an add-on
- Working with competing initiatives

Celebrating Success. Celebrating is central to supporting the progress of PLTs. Note small positive changes as well as significant milestones. Encourage teams to schedule time for celebration and also make time at schoolwide meetings to note progress. This is an opportunity to acknowledge the hard work of each team. Teamwork can be exhausting as well as exhilarating. Most teachers new to collaboration fall in love with the process and outcomes when their teamwork is focused on improving student learning. Authentic celebration can help prevent burnout and disenchantment with the essential work of each PLT.

Suggested Reading

RECOMMENDED READING FOR CHAPTER 1 ∎

Baker, P. (Ed.). (2003). Professional development that changes practice. *WCER Research Highlights, 15*(1), 1–2, 5. Madison, WI: Wisconsin Center for Education Research. Retrieved May 5, 2009, from http://www.wcer.wisc.edu/publications/highlights/ v15n1.pdf

This article provides additional detail on the six features that have been identified by research as important to providing effective professional development.

Hord, S. M. (Ed.). (2004). *Learning together, leading together: Changing schools through professional learning communities.* New York, NY: Teachers College Press.

The chapters in this book are based on research and development conducted by the Southwest Educational Development Laboratory. This book represents nine years of study and begins to document an intensive and well-controlled pattern of measurement and research of professional learning communities. The study identified five essential qualities and characteristics of professional learning communities: supportive and shared leadership; shared values and vision; collective learning and application of that learning; supportive conditions; and shared personal practice.

Hord, S. M., & Sommers, W. A. (2008). *Leading professional learning communities: Voices from research and practice.* Thousand Oaks, CA: Corwin.

The authors provide school leaders with information to guide them in developing a PLC that supports teachers and students. They cover building a vision for a PLC, implementing structures, creating policies and procedures, and developing the leadership skills required for initiating and sustaining a learning community.

McREL. (2000). *Asking the right questions: A leader's guide to systems thinking about school improvement.* Aurora, CO: Mid-Continent Research for Education and Learning.

Available at http://www.mcrel.org/PDF/SchoolImprovementReform/5982TG_AskingRight Questions.pdf

This guide stimulates thinking and provides detailed information about school change with a focus on systems thinking. A companion toolkit is found at http://www.mcrel.org/toolkit/

National Commission on Teaching and America's Future. (1996). *What matters most: Teaching for America's future. Report of the National Commission on Teaching and America's Future.* New York: NY: Columbia University, Teachers College.

The members of this commission have a wide array of economic, political, and educational affiliations. In language that is clear, direct, and compelling, NCTAF's report details the issues surrounding teacher quality and their impact on student learning. The report illustrates its assertions with ample vignettes, as well as more extended stories, from the schools studied.

WestEd. (2000*). Teachers who learn, kids who achieve: A look at schools with model professional development.* San Francisco, CA: Author.

WestEd studied eight schools selected from the winners of the National Awards Program for Model Professional Development conducted by the U.S. Department of Education. The schools range from elementary to high school, urban to rural, and most have large minority populations receiving free and reduced-price lunch. Still, each school showed dramatic gains in student performance. The study found common practices in successful professional development among the eight and described them in real-life vignettes. This slim volume provides an excellent overview of what a school looks like if it is a high-performing learning community with the role of teaming as one critical component. Available in pdf or html format, or for purchase at www.wested.org.

■ RECOMMENDED READING AND ADDITIONAL RESOURCES FOR CHAPTER 2

Brewster, C., & Railsback, J. (2003). *Building trusting relationships for school improvement: Implications for principals and teachers.* Portland, OR: Northwest Regional Educational Laboratory.

Available at http://www.nwrel.org/request/2003sept/index.html

This monograph reviews research citing key components along with some obstacles to building trust in schools. Descriptions of two schools efforts at school improvement are described.

Bryk, A. S., & Schneider, B. (2002). *Trust in schools: A core resource for improvement.* New York, NY: Russell Sage Foundation.

The authors argue that the extent of trust among adults in schools is a crucial influence on how well schools work for children. They use a variety of research methods to probe the role that trust plays in the life of schools and in students' learning.

Fullan, M. (2001). *Leading in a culture of change.* San Francisco, CA: Jossey-Bass.

This book, along with Fullan's other work on school change, offers insights into the dynamics of change and presents an imaginative approach to navigating the intricacies of the change process. Drawing on current ideas and theories on the topic of effective leadership, he integrates five core competencies into this work: (1) attending to a broader moral purpose, (2) keeping on top of the change process, (3) cultivating relationships, (4) sharing knowledge, and (5) setting a vision and context for creating coherence.

Fullan, M. (2001). *The new meaning of educational change.* (3rd ed.). New York, NY: Teachers College Press.

This revised version of Fullan's 1982 edition is an updated reference for educators in the new millennium. It provides powerful insights into the complexity of reform and recommends practical strategies to effect enduring improvement.

Gordon, D. T. (2002). Fuel for reform: The importance of trust in changing schools. *Harvard Education Letter, 18*(4), 1–4.

This article summarizes some of the research from Chicago's decade of school reform detailed in Anthony Bryk and Barbara Schneider's book, *Trust in Schools: A Core Resource for Improvement* (2002). They advocate for good social relationships and contend that a high degree of *relational trust* helps make the kinds of changes that lead to higher student achievement.

Hord, S. M., Rutherford, W. L., Huling-Austin, L., & Hall, G. E. (1987). *Taking charge of change.* Alexandria, VA: Association for Supervision and Curriculum Development.

This book provides insights and understandings about school change. Using the Concerns-Based Adoption Model (CBAM), the book examines the roles and personal needs of the people involved in a change process. It includes strategies for the total management of an innovation. The first strategy provides ways to introduce change or innovation and monitor various means of implementation. The second strategy focuses on the agent of the change process: the teacher. The third strategy provides a tool for assessing the degree to which teachers are implementing the change and for evaluating progress.

National Staff Development Council

www.nsdc.org/index.cfm

This Web site contains the rationale and annotated bibliography for each of the standards for professional development as well as more detail about the main topic of each standard. The site also provides access to a staff development library with articles from NSDC publications and links to other resources.

Wilmot, W. W., & Hocker, J. L. (2001). *Interpersonal conflict* (6th ed.). New York, NY: McGraw-Hill.

This book provides detailed information on managing conflict constructively. It provides a conflict assessment guide (pp. 205–207) to help bring specific aspects of a conflict into focus and check on gaps in information about a conflict.

RECOMMENDED READING AND ■ ADDITIONAL RESOURCES FOR CHAPTER 3

Holcomb, E. L. (2004). *Getting excited about data: Combining people, passion, and proof to maximize student achievement* (2nd ed.). Thousand Oaks, CA: Corwin.

This book builds on the first edition and provides additional guidance and support for educators who are *ready, willing, and able* to explore more sophisticated uses of data. New tools and activities facilitate active engagement with data and a collaborative culture of collective responsibility for the learning of all students.

Marchant, G. J. (n.d.). *Learning assessment model project: State-of-the art evidence eased teaching.* Muncie, IN: Ball State University.

Available at http://www.aascu.org/programs/teacher/pdf/05_ballstate.pdf

This paper describes a rubric-driven method designed to assist novice teachers in using assessments and in aligning instruction and assessment with standards and best practices.

Small Schools Project

www.smallschoolsproject.org/PDFS/asking_board_for_collab_time.pdf

This Web site offers advice on how to organize a presentation when asking your school board for teacher collaboration time.

Supovitz, J. A., & Christman, J. B. (2005). Small learning communities that actually learn: Lessons for school leaders. *Phi Delta Kappan, 86*(9), 649–651.

This brief (three-page) article describes the evaluation findings from two urban districts, Philadelphia and Cincinnati. It contains succinct and useful recommendations for school leaders intent on building communities of instructional practice among their staff.

What Works Clearinghouse

www.whatworks.ed.gov

This U.S. Department of Education's Institute of Education Sciences site—which is a work in progress—aims to provide a central source of scientific evidence on what works in education. The goal is to help identify programs, products, and practices that have demonstrated positive results.

■ RECOMMENDED READING FOR CHAPTER 4

Downey, C. J. , Steffy, B. E., English, F. W., Frase, L. E., & Poston, W. K., Jr. (2004). *The three-minute classroom walk-through: Changing school supervisory practice one teacher at a time.* Thousand Oaks, CA: Corwin.

This publication guides school leaders in developing collaborative supervision and gaining the most from the classroom walk-through. It offers a practical, time-saving alternative to traditional hierarchical supervision that impacts student achievement by cultivating self-reliant teachers who are continually improving their practice.

Drago-Severson, E. (2007). Helping teachers learn: Principals as professional development leaders. *Teachers College Record, 109*(1), 70–125.

This study describes four mutually reinforcing initiatives aimed at supporting adult learning in schools, including (1) teaming and partnering with colleagues within and outside the school, (2) providing teachers with opportunities to take on leadership roles, (3) engaging in collegial inquiry, and (4) mentoring.

Fink, E., & Resnick, L. B. (1999). *Developing principals as instructional leaders.* Pittsburgh, PA: University of Pittsburgh, Learning Research and Development Center, High Performance Learning Communities Project. Retrieved October 19, 2005, from http://www.lrdc .pitt.edu/hplc/Publications/FinkResnick.PDF

In this paper, Fink and Resnick draw on the success of an 11-year program of school improvement begun in 1987 to show how school principals established a culture of learning and raised student achievement. The authors draw the distinction between the administrative duties and instructional leadership duties of school principals; examine methods of effective organized support for school principals in their role as instructional leaders; reflect on organizational conditions that led to districtwide school improvement in a diverse urban setting in New York City's Community School District Two; and report on a strong record of successful school improvement, where teaching and learning are "what everyone talks about."

Fullan, M. (2001). *Leading in a culture of change.* San Francisco, CA: Jossey-Bass.

Many leaders face new and daunting challenges, and they must develop the skills needed to lead effectively under rapidly changing conditions. Fullan provides insights into the dynamics of change along with an imaginative approach for navigating the intricacies of the change process. He also shows how leaders can focus on certain key change themes that allow them to lead effectively under messy conditions. Finally, the book demonstrates how leaders foster leadership in others in order to build organizational capacity.

Fullan, M. (2005). *Leadership sustainability: Systems thinkers in action.* Thousand Oaks, CA: Corwin.

Building on his prior work, *The Moral Imperative of School Leadership,* Michael Fullan confronts the question: How do you develop and sustain a greater number of system thinkers in action? These proactive thinkers are the ones to bring about deeper reform while helping to produce other theoreticians working on the same issue. Fullan defines an agenda for the system thinker in action as he examines what leaders at all levels of the educational system can do to pave the way for large-scale, sustainable reform.

Hargreaves, A., & Fink, D. (2006). *Sustainable leadership.* San Francisco, CA: Jossey-Bass.

The authors set out a compelling framework of seven principles for sustainable leadership characterized by depth of learning and real achievement rather than superficially tested performance; length of impact over the long haul, beyond individual leaders, through effectively managed succession; breadth of influence, where leadership becomes a distributed responsibility; justice in ensuring that leadership actions do no harm to and actively benefit students in other schools; diversity that replaces standardization and alignment with diversity and cohesion; resourcefulness that conserves and renews leaders' energy and doesn't burn them out; and conservation that builds on the best of the past to create an even better future.

Lieberman, A., & Miller, L. (2004). *Teacher leadership.* San Francisco, CA: Jossey-Bass.

This volume in the Jossey-Bass Leadership Library in Education recognizes all teachers as leaders. It describes and provides a rationale for the emerging role of teacher leaders and their ability to make a difference in education. The authors offer case studies of innovative programs that provide teachers with opportunities to lead within their professional communities. The authors also show how to develop learning communities that include rather than exclude, create knowledge rather than merely apply it, and offer challenges and support to both new and experienced teachers.

McLaughlin, M. W., & Talbert, J. E. (2006). *Building school-based teacher learning communities: Professional strategies to improve student achievement.* New York, NY: Teachers College Press.

Based on extensive evidence that school-based teacher learning communities improve student outcomes, this book lays out an agenda to develop and sustain collaborative professional cultures. Based on their research, it provides examples from real schools illustrating the process—how teacher learning communities get started, how they develop, and how requirements for their development and markers of maturity change.

Moller, G. (2004). *Building teacher leadership within a traditional school structure.* In S. M. Hord (Ed.), *Learning together, leading together: Changing schools through professional learning communities* (pp. 140–150). New York, NY: Teachers College Press.

This chapter focuses on the professional learning community (PLC) dimension of supportive and shared leadership and its relationship to emerging teacher leadership. It also focuses on the structural design of shared leadership and the principal's role and capacities that build shared leadership.

RECOMMENDED READING FOR CHAPTER 5 ■

Copland, M. A. (2003). Leadership of inquiry: Building and sustaining capacity for school improvement. *Educational Evaluation and Policy Analysis, 25*(4), 375–395.

This report by Michael Copland of the Center for Research on the Context of Teaching at Stanford University contains useful ideas to consider for those engaged in school reform. Copland describes the Bay Area School Reform Collaborative's (BASRC) theory of action, which includes the following:

- The work of improving schools must be accomplished collectively.
- Leadership for improving teaching and learning is rooted in continual inquiry into work at the school and focuses on student learning, high standards, equity, and best practices.
- Decisions around critical problems and their solutions should be made collectively and should focus on improving learning for all students.

Gardner, H. (2006). *Changing minds: The art and science of changing our own and other people's minds.* Boston, MA: Harvard Business School Press.

Howard Gardner examines how politicians, creative artists, business leaders, teachers, and prospective dates go about the business of changing deeply held opinions—what works, what doesn't, and why.

Jolly, A. (2005). *A facilitator's guide to professional learning teams: Creating on-the-job opportunities for teachers to learn and grow.* Greensboro, NC: University of North Carolina at Greensboro, SERVE.

Jolly, A. (2008). *Team to teach: A facilitator's guide to professional learning teams.* Oxford, OH: National Staff Development Council.

This guidebook, revised in 2008, provides a set of tools for implementing PLTs with an entire faculty or part of a faculty. The book is organized in 10 chapters, each one featuring a variety of tools to use while establishing, maintaining, and evaluating a specific part of the learning team process.

Knapp, M. S., Copland, M. A., Ford, B., Markholt, A., McLaughlin, M. W., Milliken, M., et al. (2003). *Leading for learning sourcebook: Concepts and examples.* Seattle, WA: University of Washington, Center for the Study of Teaching and Policy. Retrieved April 24, 2009, from http://depts.washington.edu/ctpmail/PDFs/LforL Sourcebook-02–03.pdf

Drawing on the knowledge and field experiences of more than 300 educators, this handbook suggests how leaders can become more effective when they work to improve student learning, enhance professional learning, and build systemwide supports for all participants' learning. The handbook details five ways in which school and district leaders can advance those three agendas: (1) establish a public focus on powerful, equitable learning; (2) build communities of professionals who value and support learning; (3) engage communities, policymakers, and other external groups around improved learning; (4) identify activities with the most promise for improving learning and rally people around them; and (5) establish incentives and opportunities so that leadership for learning can be shared and developed in others.

National Staff Development Council. (2000). *Learning to lead, leading to learn: Improving school quality through principal professional development.* Oxford, OH: Author.

This slim monograph defines and provides standards for instructional leadership, supports the idea of developing teachers as leaders, and recommends that the federal government, states, and local districts adopt professional development policies targeted at upgrading the leadership capabilities of principals and teachers.

Rosenholtz, S. J. (1989). *Teachers' workplace: The social organization of schools.* New York, NY: Teachers College Press.

This study of the school as workplace provides a coherent description of how school organization at the district, school, and classroom levels influences instructional practice.

Senge, P., Cambron-McCabe, N., Lucas, T., Smith, B. Dutton, J., & Kleiner, A. (2000). *Schools that learn: A fifth discipline fieldbook for educators, parents, and everyone who cares about education.* New York, NY: Doubleday.

Building on Senge's earlier work with systems theory, this book describes practices that are meeting success across the country and around the world as schools attempt to learn, grow, and reinvent themselves using the principles of organizational learning. It offers practical tools, anecdotes, and advice that people can use to help schools learn to learn.

References

Achinstein, B. (2002a). *Community, diversity, and conflict among school teachers: The ties that blind*. New York, NY: Teachers College Press.

Achinstein, B. (2002b). Conflict amid community: The micropolitics of teacher collaboration. *Teachers College Record, 104*(3), 421–455.

Bodilly, S., & Berends, M. (1999). Necessary district support for comprehensive school reform. In G. Orfield & E.H. DeBray (Eds.), *Hard work for good schools: Fact not fads in Title I reform* (pp. 113–121). Cambridge, MA: Harvard University, Civil Rights Project. (ERIC ED447247)

Boethel, M. (2003). *Diversity: School, family, & community connections* [Annual synthesis]. Austin, TX: Southwest Educational Development Laboratory. Retrieved October 20, 2005, from http://www .sedl.org/connections/resources/diversity-synthesis.pdf

Borko, H. (2004). Professional development and teacher learning: Mapping the terrain. *Educational Researcher, 33*(8), 3–15.

Bransford, J. D., Brown, A. L., & Cocking, R. R. (Eds.). (2000). *How people learn: Brain, mind, experience, and school* (Expanded ed.). Washington, DC: National Academy Press.

Bryk, A. S., & Schneider, B. (2002). *Trust in schools: A core resource for improvement*. New York, NY: Russell Sage Foundation.

Caine, R. N., & Caine, G. (1994). *Making connections: Teaching and the human brain*. Menlo Park, CA: Addison-Wesley.

Calhoun, E. F. (1994). *How to use action research in the self-renewing school*. Alexandria, VA: Association for Supervision and Curriculum Development.

Center for Classroom Teaching and Learning. (n.d.). *Lesson study* [Web site]. Portland, OR: Northwest Regional Educational Laboratory. Retrieved May 6, 2009, from http://www.nwrel.org/lessonstudy/

Cibulka, J., & Nakayama, M. (2000). *Practitioners guide to learning communities*. Washington, DC: U.S. Department of Education, National Partnership for Excellence and Accountability in Teaching. (ERIC ED449141).

Cleveland Initiative for Education. (2004). *Effective school leadership: Adopting a systemic approach*. Cleveland, OH: Author.

Cochran-Smith, M., & Lytle, S. L. (1999). Relationships of knowledge and practice: Teacher learning in communities. In A. Iran-Nejad & P. D. Pearson (Eds.), *Review of research in education: Vol. 24* (pp. 249–305). Washington, DC: American Educational Research Association.

Cohen, D. K., & Hill, H. C. (1998). *Instructional policy and classroom performance: The mathematics reform in California* (CPRE Research Rep. No. RR-39). Philadelphia, PA: University of Pennsylvania, Consortium for Policy Research in Education.

Columbia University, Teachers College, Lesson Study Research Group. (n.d.). *What is lesson study?* Retrieved May 6, 2009, from http://www.tc.edu/lessonstudy/lesson study.html

Cook, C. J., & Fine, C. (1997). *Critical issues: Finding time for professional development*. Oak Brook, IL: North Central Regional Educational Laboratory, Midwest Consortium for Mathematics and Science Education. Retrieved April 17, 2009, from http://www.ncrel. org/sdrs/areas/issues/educatrs/profdevl/pd300.htm

Copland, M. A. (2003). Leadership of inquiry: Building and sustaining capacity for school improvement. *Educational Evaluation and Policy Analysis, 25*(4), 375–395.

Cotton, K. (2003). *Principals and student achievement: What the research says*. Portland, OR: Northwest Regional Educational Laboratory, & Alexandria, VA: Association for Supervision and Curriculum Development.

Curry, M. (2008). Critical friends groups: The possibilities and limitations embedded in teacher professional communities aimed at instructional improvement and school reform. *Teachers College Record, 110*(4), 733–774.

Daniels, H., Bizar, M., & Zemelman, S. (2001). *Rethinking high school: Best practice in teaching, learning, and leadership*. Portsmouth, NH: Heinemann.

Darling-Hammond, L. (1996). What matters most: A competent teacher for every child. *Phi Delta Kappan, 78*(3), 193–200.

Darling-Hammond, L. (1998). Teachers and teaching: Testing policy hypotheses from a national commission report. *Educational Researcher, 27*(1), 5–15.

Darling-Hammond, L. (1999). *Teacher quality and student achievement: A review of state policy evidence.* Seattle, WA: University of Washington, Center for the Study of Teaching and Policy. Retrieved May 6, 2009, from http://depts.washington.edu/ctpmail/PDFs/ LDH_1999.pdf

Davis, S., Darling-Hammond, L., LaPointe, M., & Meyerson, D. (2005). *School leadership study: Developing successful principals.* Stanford, CA: Stanford University, Stanford Educational Leadership Institute. Retrieved October 20, 2005, from http://www.gsb. stanford.edu/csi/pdf/SELI_sls_research_review.pdf

Deal, T. E., & Peterson, K. D. (1999). *Shaping school culture: The heart of leadership.* San Francisco, CA: Jossey-Bass.

Desimone, L. M., Porter, A. C., Garet, M. S., Yoon, K. S., & Birman, B. F. (2002). Effects of professional development on teachers' instruction: Results from a three-year longitudinal study. *Educational Evaluation and Policy Analysis, 24*(2), 81–112.

Downey, C. J., Steffy, B. E., English, F. W., Frase, L. E., & Poston, W. K., Jr. (2004). *The three-minute classroom walkthrough: Changing school supervisory practice one teacher at a time.* Thousand Oaks, CA: Corwin.

DuFour, R. P. (1998). Why celebrate? *Journal of Staff Development, 19*(4), 58–59.

DuFour, R. P., & Eaker, R. (1998). *Professional learning communities at work: Best practices for enhancing student achievement.* Bloomington, IN: National Educational Service.

Eaker, R., DuFour, R. P., & DuFour, R. B. (2002). *Getting started: Reculturing schools to become professional learning communities.* Bloomington, IN: National Educational Service.

Fager, J. (1997). *Scheduling alternatives: Options for student success.* Portland, OR: Northwest Regional Educational Laboratory. Retrieved April 3, 2009, from http://www.nwrel. org/request/feb97/index.html

Featherstone, H. (1991). The rewards of a four-day school week. *Principal, 71*(1), 28–30.

Ferrance, E. (2000). *Action research.* Providence, RI: Brown University, Education Alliance, Northeast and Islands Regional Educational Laboratory. Retrieved May 6, 2009, from http://www.alliance.brown.edu/pubs/ themes_ed/act_research.pdf

Fink, E., & Resnick, L. B. (1999). *Developing principals as instructional leaders.* Pittsburgh, PA: University of Pittsburgh, Learning Research and Development Center, High Performance Learning Communities Project. Retrieved April 3, 2009, from http://www.lrdc.pitt.edu/hplc/Publications/FinkResnick.PDF

Fleming, G. L. (2004). Principals and teachers as continuous learners. In S. M. Hord (Ed.), *Learning together, leading together: Changing schools through professional learning communities* (pp. 20–30). New York, NY: Teachers College Press.

Fleming, G. L., & Thompson, T. L. (2004). The role of trust building and its relation to collective responsibility. In S.M. Hord (Ed.), *Learning together, leading together: Changing schools through professional learning communities* (pp. 31–44). New York, NY: Teachers College Press.

Fulford, N. (1994). *Professional development: Changing times* (NCREL Policy Brief No. 4). Naperville, IL: North Central Regional Educational Laboratory. (ERIC ED376618)

Fullan, M. G. (with Stiegelbauer, S.). (1991). *The new meaning of educational change* (2nd ed.). New York, NY: Teachers College Press.

Fullan, M. G. (2001a). *The new meaning of educational change* (3rd ed.). New York, NY: Teachers College Press.

Fullan, M. (2001b). *Leading in a culture of change.* San Francisco, CA: Jossey-Bass.

Fullan, M. (2005). *Leadership and sustainability: System thinkers in action.* Thousand Oaks, CA: Corwin.

Gardner, H. (2006). *Changing minds: The art and science of changing our own and other people's minds.* Boston, MA: Harvard Business School Press.

Garet, M. S., Birman, B. F., Porter, A. C., Desimone, L., & Herman, R. (with Yoon, K. S.). (1999). *Designing effective professional development: Lessons from the Eisenhower Program* [Executive summary]. Washington, DC: U.S. Department of Education, Office of the Under Secretary. Retrieved April 3, 2009, from http://www.ed .gov/inits/teachers/ eisenhower/execsum/index.html

Garet, M., Porter, A., Desimone, L., Birman, B., & Yoon, K. (2001). What makes professional development effective? Analysis of a national sample of teachers. *American Educational Research Journal, 8*(4), 915–945.

Hall, G. E., & Hord, S. M. (2001). *Implementing change: Patterns, principles, and potholes.* Boston, MA: Allyn & Bacon.

Hall, G., & Hord, S. (2006). *Implementing change: Patterns, principles, and potholes.* Needham Heights, MA: Allyn & Bacon.

Hargreaves, A., & Fink, D. (2006). *Sustainable leadership.* San Francisco, CA: Jossey-Bass.

Hawley, W. D., & Valli, L. (1999). The essentials of effective professional development: A new consensus. In L. Darling-Hammond & G. Sykes (Eds.), *Teaching as the learning profession: Handbook of policy and practice* (pp. 127–150). San Francisco, CA: Jossey-Bass.

Hirsh, S. (2003, March). Resolving conflicts key to collaboration. *Results.* Oxford, OH: National Staff Development Council. Retrieved April 24, 2009, from http://www.nsdc. org/news/results/res3-03hirs.cfm

Hord, S. M. (1997). *Professional learning communities: Communities of continuous inquiry and improvement.* Austin, TX: Southwest Educational Development Laboratory. Retrieved May 6, 2009, from http://www .sedl.org/pubs/change34/plc-cha34.pdf

Hord, S. M. (Ed.). (2004). *Learning together, leading together: Changing schools through professional learning communities.* New York, NY: Teachers College Press.

Hord, S. M., Rutherford, W. L., Huling-Austin, L., & Hall, G. E. (1987). *Taking charge of change.* Alexandria, VA: Association for Supervision and Curriculum Development.

Hord, S. M., & Sommers, W. A. (2008). *Leading professional learning communities: Voices from research and practice.* Thousand Oaks, CA: Corwin.

Jalongo, M. R. (1991). *Creating learning communities: The role of the teacher in the 21st century.* Bloomington, IN: National Educational Service.

Johnson, D. W., & Johnson, F. P. (1994). *Joining together: Group theory and group skills* (5th ed.). Boston, MA: Allyn & Bacon.

Joyce, B. (2004). How are professional learning communities created? History has a few messages [Discussion of Tipping Point by Mike Schmoker]. *Phi Delta Kappan, 86*(1), 76–83.

Joyce, B. & Showers, B. (2002). *Student achievement through staff development.* Alexandria, VA: Association for Supervision and Curriculum Development.

Katzenbach, J. R., & Smith, D. K. (1999). *The wisdom of teams: Creating the high-performance organization.* New York, NY: HarperBusiness.

Katzenmeyer, M., & Moller, G. (1996). *Awakening the sleeping giant: Leadership development for teachers.* Thousand Oaks, CA: Corwin.

Kennedy, M. (1998). *Form and substance in inservice teacher education* (Research Monograph No. 13). Madison, WI: University of Wisconsin, National Institute for Science Education.

King, B. M., & Newmann, F. M. (2000). Will teacher learning advance school goals? *Phi Delta Kappan, 81*(8), 576–580.

Knapp, M. S., Copland, M. A., Ford, B., Markholt, A., McLaughlin, M. W., Milliken, M., et al. (2003). *Leading for learning sourcebook: Concepts and examples.* Seattle, WA: University of Washington, Center for the Study of Teaching and Policy. Retrieved April 24, 2009, from http://depts.washington.edu/ctpmail/PDFs/LforL Sourcebook-02-03.pdf

Kruger, R., Woo, A., Miller, B., Davis, D., & Rayborn, R. (2008). *Washington State Board of Education: Study of state and local barriers to raising achievement dramatically for all students. Final report.* Portland, OR: Northwest Regional Educational Laboratory.

Lambert, L. (2003). *Leadership capacity for lasting school improvement.* Alexandria, VA: Association for Supervision and Curriculum Development.

Lee, V. E., & Smith, J. B. (1995). Effects of high school restructuring and size on early gains in achievement and engagement. *Sociology of Education, 68*(4), 241–270.

Lee, V. E., & Smith, J. B. (1996). Collective responsibility for learning and its effects on gains in achievement for early secondary school students. *American Journal of Education, 104*(2), 103–147.

Lee, V. E., Smith, J. B., & Croninger, R. G. (1997). How high school organization influences the equitable distribution of learning in mathematics and science. *Sociology of Education, 70*(2), 128–150.

Leffler, J. C. (2008). [Survey of educational needs in five Northwest states]. Unpublished raw data.

Leithwood, K., Louis, K. S., Anderson, S., & Wahlstrom, K. (2004). *Review of research: How leadership influences student learning.* Minneapolis, MN: University of Minnesota, Center for Applied Research and Educational Improvement, & Toronto, Ontario, Canada: University of Toronto, Ontario Institute for Studies in Education.

Lewis, A. (2000). *Revisioning professional development: What learner-centered professional development looks like.* Washington, DC: U.S. Department of Education, National Partnership for Excellence and Accountability in Teaching. (ERIC ED443806)

Lewis, L., Parsad, B., Carey, N., Bartfai, N., Farris, E., Smerdon, B., et al. (1999). *Teacher quality: A report on the preparation and qualifications of public school teachers* [Statistical analysis rep.]. Washington, DC: U.S. Department of Education, National Center for Education Statistics. Retrieved April 27, 2008, from http://nces.ed.gov/pubsearch/pubsinfo.asp? pubid=1999080

Lieberman, A., & Miller, L. (2000). Teaching and teacher development: A new synthesis for a new century. In R.S. Brandt (Ed.), *Education in a new era* (pp. 47–63). Alexandria, VA: Association for Supervision and Curriculum Development.

Lieberman, A., & Miller, L. (2004). *Teacher leadership.* San Francisco, CA: Jossey-Bass.

Little, J. W. (1981, April). *The power of organizational setting: School norms and staff development*. Paper presented at the annual meeting of the American Educational Research Association, Los Angeles, CA. (ERIC ED221918)

Little, J. W. (1982). Norms of collegiality and experimentation: Workplace conditions of school success. *American Education Research Journal, 19*(3), 325–340.

Little, J. W. (2002). Locating learning in teachers' communities of practice: Opening up problems of analysis in records of everyday practice. *Teaching and Teacher Education, 18*(8), 917–946.

Louis, K. S., & Miles, M. B. (1990). *Improving the urban high school: What works and why*. New York, NY: Teachers College Press.

Maeroff, G. I. (1993). *Team building for school change: Equipping teachers for new roles*. New York, NY: Teachers College Press.

Mayer, D. P., Mullens, J. E., Moore, M. T., & Ralph, J. (2000). *Monitoring school quality: An indicators report*. Washington, DC: U. S. Department of Education, National Center for Education Statistics. Retrieved April 24, 2009, from http://nces.ed.gov/pubsearch/ pubsinfo.asp?pubid=2001030

McLaughlin, M. W., & Talbert, J. E. (1993). *Contexts that matter for teaching and learning: Strategic opportunities for meeting the nation's education goals*. Stanford, CA: Stanford University, Center for Research on the Context of Secondary School Teaching.

McLaughlin, M. W., & Talbert, J. E. (2001). *Professional communities and the work of high school teaching*. Chicago, IL: University of Chicago Press.

McLaughlin, M. W., & Talbert, J. E. (2003). *Reforming districts: How districts support school reform. A research report*. Seattle, WA: University of Washington, Center for the Study of Teaching and Policy. Retrieved April 27, 2009, from http://depts.washington .edu/ctpmail/PDFs/ReformingDistricts-09-2003.pdf

McLaughlin, M. W., & Talbert, J. E. (2006). *Building school-based teacher learning communities: Professional strategies to improve student achievement*. New York, NY: Teachers College Press.

McMackin, M. C., & Witherell, N. L. (2005). Different routes to the same destination: Drawing conclusions with tiered graphic organizers. *The Reading Teacher, (50)*, 241–252.

McTighe, J. (2008). Making the most of professional learning communities. *Learning Principal, 3*(8), 1, 4–7. Oxford, OH: National Staff Development Council.

Milliken, M., Ross, P., Pecheone, R., & Darling-Hammond, L. (2006). *District office support of high school design: Ten challenges*. Manuscript in preparation, Stanford University, CA. Retrieved April 24, 2009, from http://www.srnleads.org/data/ pdfs/ten_prepub.pdf

Moller, G. (2004). Building teacher leadership within a traditional school structure. In S.M. Hord (Ed.), *Learning together, leading together: Changing schools through professional learning communities* (pp. 140–150). New York, NY: Teachers College Press.

Morrissey, M. S., & Cowan, D. (2000, April). *Creating and sustaining a professional learning community: Actions and perceptions of leadership*. Paper presented at the annual meeting of the American Educational Research Association, New Orleans, LA.

Murphy, C. (1997). Finding time for faculties to study together. *Journal of Staff Development, 18*(3), 29–32.

Murphy, C. U., & Lick, D. W. (1998). *Whole faculty study groups: A powerful way to change schools and enhance learning*. Thousand Oaks, CA: Corwin.

Murphy, C. U., & Lick, D. W. (2001). *Whole faculty study groups: Creating student-based professional development* (2nd ed.). Thousand Oaks, CA: Corwin.

National Association of Elementary School Principals. (2001). *Leading learning communities: NAESP standards for what principals should know and be able to do*. Alexandria, VA: Author.

National Commission on Teaching and America's Future. (1996). *What matters most: Teaching for America's future. Report of the National Commission on Teaching and America's Future*. New York, NY: Columbia University, Teachers College.

National Education Commission on Time and Learning. (1994). *Prisoners of time: Report of the National Education Commission on Time and Learning*. Washington, DC: Author. Retrieved April 25, 2009, from http://www .ed.gov/pubs/PrisonersOfTime/ index.html

National Institute for Urban School Improvement. (2001). *On point . . . On time and how to get more of it. Brief discussions of critical issues in urban education*. Newton, MA: Education Development Center. (ERIC ED455344)

National Staff Development Council. (2000). *Learning to lead, leading to learn: Improving school quality through principal professional development*. Oxford, OH: Author.

National Staff Development Council. (2001). *NSDC standards for staff development* (Rev. ed.). Oxford, OH: Author. Retrieved April 24, 2009, from http://www.nsdc.org/stan dards/ index.cfm

Nave, B. (2000). *Critical friends groups: Their impact on students, teachers, and schools*. Bloomington, IN: Annenberg Institute for School Reform.

Pankake, A. M. (1998). *Implementation: Making things happen*. Larchmont, NY: Eye on Education.

Porter, A. C., Garet, M. S., Desimone, L., Yoon, K. S., & Birman, B. F. (2000). *Does professional development change teaching practice? Results from a three-year study.* Washington, DC: U. S. Department of Education, Planning and Evaluation Service. Retrieved May 6, 2009, from http://www.ed.gov/rschstat/eval/teaching/epdp/report.pdf

Raphael, J. (2005). *Report on results from formative field test for professional learning team project.* Portland, OR: Northwest Regional Educational Laboratory.

Raywid, M. A. (1993). Finding time for collaboration. *Educational Leadership, 51*(1), 30–34.

Reeves, D. B. (2003). The data quandary: Which to use—year-to-year or cohort? *Focus on Achievement, 5*(2), 1–2.

Reeves, D. B. (2004). *Accountability for learning: How teachers and school leaders can take charge.* Alexandria, VA: Association for Supervision and Curriculum Development.

Richardson, V., & Placier, P. (2001). Teacher change. In V. Richardson (Ed.), *Handbook of research on teaching* (4th ed., pp. 905–947). Washington, DC: American Educational Research Association.

Rosenholtz, S. J. (1989). *Teachers' workplace: The social organization of schools.* New York, NY: Longman.

Sather, S. E. (2004). *The Spokane School District: Intentionally building capacity that leads to increased student achievement.* Portland, OR: Northwest Regional Educational Laboratory.

Schmoker, M. (1996). *Results: The key to continuous school improvement.* Alexandria, VA: Association for Supervision and Curriculum Development.

Schmoker, M. (2004). Tipping point: From feckless reform to substantive instructional improvement. *Phi Delta Kappan, 85*(6), 424–432.

Schmuck, R. A., & Runkel, P. J. (1994). *The handbook of organization development in schools and colleges* (4th ed.). Prospect Heights, IL: Waveland Press.

Senge, P. M. (1990). *The fifth discipline: The art and practice of the learning organization.* New York, NY: Doubleday/Currency.

Senge, P. M., Cambron-McCabe, N., Lucas, T., Smith, B., Dutton, J., & Kleiner, A. (2000). *Schools that learn: A fifth discipline fieldbook for educators, parents, and everyone who cares about education.* New York, NY: Doubleday.

Senge, P. M., Kleiner, A., Roberts, C., Ross, R. B., & Smith, B. J. (1994). *The fifth discipline fieldbook: Strategies and tools for building a learning organization.* New York, NY: Doubleday.

Showers, B., Joyce, B. R., & Bennett, B. (1987). Synthesis of research on staff development: A framework for future study and a state-of-the-art analysis. *Educational Leadership, 45*(3), 77–87.

Small Schools Project. *Asking your school board for teacher collaboration time.* Retrieved April 29, 2009, from http://www.smalsshcoolsproject.org/PDFS/asking_board_for_col lab_time.pdf

Smylie, M. A., Allensworth, E., Greenberg, R. C., Harris, R., & Luppescu, S. (2001). *Teacher professional development in Chicago: Supporting effective practice.* Chicago, IL: University of Chicago, Consortium on Chicago School Research. Retrieved April 25, 2009, from http://ccsr.uchicago.edu/publications/p0d01.pdf

Sparks, D., & Hirsch, S. (2000). *A national plan for improving professional development.* Oxford, OH: National Staff Development Council. (ERIC ED442779)

Spillane, J. P., Halverson, R., & Diamond, J. B. (2001). Investigating school leadership practice: A distributed perspective. *Educational Researcher, 30*(3), 23–28.

Stigler, J. W., & Hiebert, J. (1999). *The teaching gap: Best ideas from the world's teachers for improving education in the classroom.* New York, NY: Free Press.

Supovitz, J. A. (2002). Developing communities of instructional practice. *Teachers College Record, 104*(8), 1591–1626.

Supovitz, J. A., & Christman, J. B. (2003). *Developing communities of instructional practice: Lessons from Cincinnati and Philadelphia.* (CPRE Policy Brief No. RB-39). Philadelphia, PA: University of Pennsylvania, Consortium for Policy Research in Education. Retrieved May 6, 2009, from http://www.cpre.org/images/stories/cpre_pdfs/rb39.pdf

Supovitz, J. A., & Christman, J. B. (2005). Small learning communities that actually learn: Lessons for school leaders. *Phi Delta Kappan, 86*(9), 649–651.

Togneri, W., & Anderson, S. E. (2003). *Beyond islands of excellence: What districts can do to improve instruction and achievement in all schools.* Washington, DC: Learning First Alliance.

Uline, C. L., Tschannen-Moran, M., & Perez, L. (2003). Constructive conflict: How controversy can contribute to school improvement. *Teachers College Record, 105*(5), 782–816.

U.S. Department of Education. (2004). *New No Child Left Behind flexibility: Highly qualified teachers* [Fact sheet]. Washington, DC: Author. Retrieved April 27, 2009, from http://www.ed.gov/nclb/methods/teachers/hqtflexibility.html

U.S. Department of Education. (2005). *New No Child Left Behind flexibility: Highly qualified teachers* [Fact sheet]. Washington, DC: Author. Retrieved October 17, 2005, from www.ed.gov/nclb/methods/teachers/hqtflexibility.html

Vescio, V., Ross, D., & Adams, A. (2006, January). *A review of research on professional learning communities: What do we know?* Paper presented at the National School Reform Faculty Research Forum, Denver, CO. Retrieved May 6, 2009, from http://www.nsrfharmony.org/research.vescio_ross_adams.pdf

Vescio, V., Ross, D., & Adams, A. (2008). A review of research on the impact of professional learning communities on teaching practice and student learning. *Teaching and Teacher Education, 24*(1), 80–91.

Wald, P. J., & Castleberry, M. S. (Eds.). (1999). *Realigning our schools: Building professional learning communities.* Washington, DC: George Washington University. (ERIC ED427478)

Waters, T., Marzano, R. J., & McNulty, B. (2003). *Balanced leadership: What 30 years of research tells us about the effect of leadership on student achievement* [Working paper]. Aurora, CO: Mid-continent Research for Education and Learning. Retrieved April 25, 2009, from http://www.mcrel.org/products/144/

Watts, G. D., & Castle, S. (1993). The time dilemma in school restructuring. *Phi Delta Kappan, 75*(4), 306–310.

Wenglinsky, H. (2000). *How teaching matters: Bringing the classroom back into discussions of teacher quality.* Princeton, NJ: Educational Testing Service, Policy Information Center. Retrieved May 6, 2009, from http://www.mff.org/pubs/ets_mff_study2000.pdf

WestEd. (2000). *Teachers who learn, kids who achieve: A look at schools with model professional development.* San Francisco, CA: Author.

Wilmot, W. W., & Hocker, J. L. (2001). *Interpersonal conflict* (6th ed.). New York, NY: McGraw-Hill.

Wood, F. H., & Thompson, S. R. (1993). Assumptions about staff development based on research and best practice. *Journal of Staff Development, 14*(4), 52–57.

Index

CORWIN
A SAGE Company

The Corwin logo—a raven striding across an open book—represents the union of courage and learning. Corwin is committed to improving education for all learners by publishing books and other professional development resources for those serving the field of PreK–12 education. By providing practical, hands-on materials, Corwin continues to carry out the promise of its motto: **"Helping Educators Do Their Work Better."**

AMERICAN ASSOCIATION OF SCHOOL ADMINISTRATORS

The American Association of School Administrators, founded in 1865, is the professional organization for more than 13,000 educational leaders across the United States. AASA's mission is to support and develop effective school system leaders who are dedicated to the highest quality public education for all children. For more information, visit www.aasa.org.

education northwest

Education Northwest, formerly known as the Northwest Regional Educational Laboratory, is a nonprofit organization dedicated to transforming teaching and learning. We work with educators, administrators, policymakers, and communities across the country. Headquartered in Portland, Oregon, our mission is to improve learning by building capacity in schools, families, and communities through applied research and development. More information about Education Northwest is available at www.educationnorthwest.org